CHILDREN'S PARTIES

CHILDREN'S PARTIES

ANGELA WILKES

DK

DORLING KINDERSLEY

LONDON • NEW YORK • STUTTGART • MOSCOW

A DORLING KINDERSLEY BOOK

Editor
Caroline Greene/Annelise Evans

Designers
Emma Boys/Tracey Clarke

Art Editor
Karen Ward

Managing Editor
Jemima Dunne/Maureen Rissik

Managing Art Editor
Philip Gilderdale

DTP Designer
Karen Ruane

Production
Maryann Rogers

Photography
Susanna Price
Tim Ridley
Clive Streeter

First published in Great Britain in 1996 by
Dorling Kindersley Limited,
9 Henrietta Street, London WC2E 8PS
Copyright © 1996 Dorling Kindersley Limited, London
Text copyright © 1996 Angela Wilkes

A CIP catalogue record for the book is available from
the British Library.

ISBN 0 7513 0178 7

Reproduced in Hong Kong by Bright Arts
Printed and bound by Star Standard Industries, Singapore

Publisher's Note
Throughout this book, the pronouns "she" and "he" refer to both
sexes, except where a topic applies specifically to a girl or boy.
The term "parents" refers to parents, a parent, or a guardian.

CONTENTS

PARTY PLANNING

Careful preparation will make a party a happy occasion for the guests and a trouble-free experience for you.

Planning a Party for a 1- or 2-year-old
Parties for babies and toddlers should be short and simple.

———————————

Planning a Party for a 3-year-old
Three-year-olds enjoy action rhymes and simple musical games.

———————————

Planning a Party for a 4-year-old
Children of this age throw themselves into enjoying a simple party theme and a wider range of games and activities.

———————————

Planning a Party for a 5-year-old
Five-year-olds very much like a theme and a wide variety of games, so plan enough to keep the party going with a swing.

———————————

Planning a Party for Mixed Ages
Advice on keeping a mixed group of children amused.

———————————

Troubleshooting
How to smooth over trouble spots during and after the party.

PARTY PLANNING TIPS

◊ Keep the party short and the number of guests small.

◊ Post invitations (pages 28–29) in plenty of time. Supervise your child handing them out at school, or you may have many unexpected guests.

◊ Plan everything well ahead of the party: the venue, the guests, the decorations, menu, games, activities, props, and treats. For reference, keep lists of all you will need.

◊ Don't be too ambitious. Keep the party simple, with one special activity or feature. Most small children have very short attention spans.

◊ Involve the birthday child as much as possible in the preparations, but don't press a reluctant child.

◊ For a party at home, decide which areas of the house or garden will be out of bounds to small guests.

◊ For an outing, keep the party small and take along several helpers. An outing can be as simple as a picnic in the park, or a football game with tea back at home. It could be a trip to a zoo, swimming pool, or cinema.

◊ If you hire a party venue, book well in advance. Check if supervision is provided and confirm the booking in writing. Ring a few days before the party to check that all is in order.

◊ Write out a party plan, with the games in order of play. Remember, children may only spend 20–30 minutes eating the party meal.

◊ Arrange to have at least one adult helper who knows your child. For a toddler's party, you may need several helpers; ask some of the parents.

◊ Pin your party plan in an obvious place, so you and your helper can refer to it when needed.

◊ Arrange all your props, goody bags, and music tapes in boxes beforehand and tell your helper where they are.

◊ Shut away pets, such as dogs, that may frighten or hurt young children.

◊ Keep a list of the guests' home telephone numbers to hand, in case of upsets or emergencies.

◊ Tell guests where to leave their coats and where the lavatory is.

PLANNING A PARTY
FOR A
1- OR 2-YEAR-OLD

Very young children do not understand what a party is, so a first or second birthday party will be a special celebration for family and friends at which the child simply enjoys the fun.

Two-year-old
He is still vague about birthdays.

Cheesy shapes
(page 57)

Concertina invitation
Toddlers find these simple shapes
(page 28) fascinating to play with.

Soft toys
These make ideal playthings or going-home gifts.

One-year-old
Supply plenty of cushions and bright, chunky toys.

Guests
For a first birthday party, you may want to ask a few relations, but remember a baby can be over-awed by a large group. Otherwise, have a joint party with two or three friends who have babies of the same age. For two-year-olds, you could invite four or five children and their parents. Plan a lunch or tea party of 1–1½ hours.

Invitations
Choose bold colours and strong shapes, like a favourite animal, for invitations. Cut-outs (page 28) are fun: thread a ribbon through the top of each one so that guests can hang them up in their bedrooms.

Decorations
Keep these simple: hang a few bright streamers out of reach. Don't use balloons, they may frighten young children and are a choking hazard when deflated.

The table is the focus of the party, so use a paper tablecloth, napkins, and plates with a jolly party design, and include settings for the parents. For two-year-old's party, you could set out a child-sized table and small chairs. Ask the parents to bring their child's drinking bottle or beaker.

Menu
Babies and toddlers like to pick at party finger foods and drink a large amount, so aim to provide a few tiny tempting goodies (pages 54–69) in soft and crisp textures, such as: tiny sandwiches, finger food, like cucumber sticks or carrot sticks softened by blanching, pastry shapes, picture biscuits, mini cupcakes, small portions of ice cream, birthday cake, plenty of milk or diluted fruit juice.

Adult guests may eat some of the finger food with the children, but provide extra refreshments for adult tastes. Try open sandwiches, canapés, sparkling fruit punch, and fruit fools.

Toys
One-year-olds don't yet play together but often play alongside each other with separate toys. Put plenty of cushions on the floor and lay out board books, soft toys, balls, rattles, and chunky building blocks. Add bigger toys with wheels (cars, trucks, trains) for toddlers. For a toddler's summer party, set out a low climbing frame or mini-slide in the garden, and put out small tricycles and pedal cars for the children to play with.

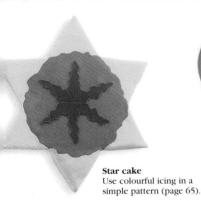

Star cake
Use colourful icing in a simple pattern (page 65).

Finger food
Serve crunchy titbits for the children and add savoury dips for the parents (page 54).

Playtime

here is no need to organize games or this age group, as they are happy st to play with toys. They do enjoy little musical entertainment, owever. Have a cassette player eady with nursery-rhyme tapes, so at children can dance if they want . With two-year-olds, try a few ction songs, such as Here We Go ound the Mulberry Bush (page 38), or Musical Bumps (page 42). Make a few basic instruments (page 43) and have a musical procession all through the house or garden.

Ring-a-ring-a-roses
Toddlers, as well as older children, enjoy joining in with action songs (page 38-39).

Going-home treats

or each child, wrap a small gift in a ound bag of coloured tissue paper r wrapping paper (page 35). Choose mall toys that are safety-approved or children under three years old.
  You could give one-year-olds ifferent board books or bath books, ath toys, squeaky toys, or party hats. wo-year-olds like small packs of hunky wax crayons, magic painting ooks, colourful toy animals, and ovelty bath sponges.

Two-year-old
At this age, a party is a novelty and a time to have fun.

PARTY PLAN

Keep the party simple and be prepared to adapt it if children are grumpy or need distracting.

◇ Children arrive and play with toys.

◇ Serve drinks to parents.

◇ Help birthday child to open the presents.

◇ Party meal. Take photographs or shoot a video film.

◇ Children play with books and toys, or in the garden.

◇ Musical entertainment.

◇ Going-home time and treats.

PARTY TIPS

◇ "Babyproof" the party rooms. Make sure breakable objects are out of reach and that there are no sharp corners on which to bump heads.

◇ Put up a stairgate. Put safety covers in all the floor-level sockets and tie up curtain cords.

◇ To avoid tears, put away your child's favourite toys.

◇ Do not serve any hard sweets, nuts, or small fruits to the children; they could choke.

◇ Ask a friend to serve the adults during the meal.

◇ Don't play games for too long; babies and toddlers have very short attention spans and they tire easily.

◇ Play Sleeping Lions (page 40) to calm the children down just before they go home.

PLANNING A PARTY
— FOR A —
3-YEAR-OLD

Balloons
Hang balloons
up out of reach.

By the time children are three, they are beginning to understand what parties are all about. The key elements of the party for a birthday child are "my friends, presents, and a cake with candles".

Crêpe streamers
Use bold colours
(page 30).

Concertina invitation
Choose a starry
concertina (page 28)
for a shape theme.

Hot potato
Music and a ball
combine in a
great game
(page 43).

Novelty straw
Cut out and decorate a
5cm (2in) card "face"
and slot it onto a straw.

Guests
Your child may now have special friends at a playgroup or nursery. Aim to invite no more children than will fit around your table; about six is ideal. Plan a lunch or tea party of 1½–2 hours. Most three-year-olds are not yet independent enough to stay without their parents.

Invitations
Try making concertina or cut-out invitations (page 28), keeping to a simple colour or shape theme (page 20). For example, make a spotty bear or a purple elephant. Your child can help you choose which shapes to make and can even help you decorate them.

Decorations
Decorate the party room with simple streamers and balloons out of reach of the children. You could introduce an animal theme, or colours and shapes, for this age group (pages 20–23). Focus your efforts on the party table and make it as colourful as possible. Have a decorative paper tablecloth, plates, and cups. Write the guests' names on party hats (pages 32–33), put one on each plate, and make a game of finding the right seat.

Menu
Be inventive and cut small treats into familiar animal shapes or decorate with colourful patterns.

Try these dishes (pages 54–70): small open sandwiches, cheesy shapes, tomato treats, animal-shaped crisps, mini sausages, picture biscuits, iced cupcakes, ice cream, choco-milk, and diluted fruit juices.

Make a special cake that looks like your child's favourite animal or toy (pages 62–69). Remember to provide enough food and drink for the children's parents (page 8).

Toys
Provide plenty of toys for this age group, as there are always some children who are reluctant or too shy to join in games. Three-year-olds will spend much of a party in free play, and enjoy "let's pretend". Lay out dolls and soft toys, toy cars and trains, picture books, simple jigsaws,

Feely bag
Three-year-olds can cope with
easy guessing games (page 44).

Cupcakes
Ice these and decorate
with patterns or faces (page 59).

⚠ CAUTION!
*Balloons can be a
choking hazard.*

dressing-up box, and a messy corner
with finger paints and non-toxic
modelling clay – provide overalls to
protect the children's clothes. If the
weather permits, put a low climbing
frame, sandpit, or paddling pool in
the garden. Always keep a close
eye on the children.

Games

Choose about four short and easy
games (pages 38–49). Three-year-olds
love almost any musical or copying
game. Avoid competitive games that
can lead to tears among the losers.
If you want to give treats, keep them
small and present one to every child
as a reward for their efforts. Try the
following games: any action songs
or hand rhymes, Sleeping Lions,
Mr Bear's Footsteps, Pass the Parcel,
Musical Bumps, Match the Balloon,
Follow My Leader, Roll a Ball, and
Making Bubbles.

Going-home treats

Make a colourful fabric or paper
party bag (page 35) for each child.
Fill each bag with four or five small
gifts, such as stickers, plastic farm
animals, wax crayons, wriggly snakes,
scooters, toy cars, small picture books,
or soft balls. Check that the items are
all safe for three-year-old children.

Three-year-old
A birthday party
can be very
exciting for
children of
this age.

PARTY PLAN

◊ Children arrive and spend
time in free play.

◊ Birthday child opens gifts.

◊ Serve drinks to parents.

◊ Play Follow My Leader.

◊ Action songs or hand rhymes.

◊ Party meal. Take photographs
or shoot a video film.

◊ Play two or three games.

◊ Children's free play.

◊ Party bags
and
going-
home time.

PARTY TIPS

◊ Move any breakable items or
favourite toys to a room that is
out of bounds.

◊ Enlist one or two of the
guest parents as helpers
beforehand; give them a copy
of the party plan.

◊ Ask your helpers to play
with any shy guests while you
supervise the games.

◊ Be flexible. Three-year-olds
can be temperamental and may
not want to join in organized
games at all. If so, encourage
them to play with the toys.

◊ If the children become too
boisterous, sit them down for
some hand rhymes or a really
quiet game, such as Sleeping
Lions, or read them a story.

◊ If one child is disruptive,
separate him from the others
and give him a little job to do.

PLANNING A PARTY
— FOR A —
4-YEAR-OLD

Four-year-olds are very enthusiastic about parties. Party themes and games come into their own and the birthday child will enjoy helping you to plan the festivities.

Plate mask
Make animal masks like thi bear (page 32

Mystery parcel
This guessing game (page 44) is great fun.

Dressing-up invitation
A guest can cut out this harlequin mask to wear (page 29).

Stick the Tail on the Donkey
Children always like traditional games (page 41).

Princess's hat
Make this (page 33) for a fairy-tale or kings and queens theme party.

Guests
Aim to invite six to ten guests to a party for this age group. Ask your child which friends he wants to invite to the party and only ask relations with whom the child is comfortable. You can ask parents to leave the children at the party and pick them up about two hours later, although there may be one or two children who still prefer their parents to stay with them (more helpers for you!). Make sure that you have at least one adult to help you with hosting the party.

Invitations
Children might be able to draw simple pictures by now, so why not use one of your child's drawings as a basis for techno invitations? You could make photocopies or computer printouts (page 29) and ask the child to colour them in. Alternatively, make cut-out invitations (page 28) and let the child decorate them. For a theme, send dressing-up invitations (page 29).

Decorations
Four-year-olds may have very definite ideas about the decorations or party theme, so enlist their help. Dinosaurs and monsters are popular (you could adapt the ideas on animal themes given on page 23). Cut out large animal shapes, ask your child to decorate them, and hang them on the walls. Make animal streamers (page 30) or a mobile (page 31) to hang above the table. Match the table decorations to the theme and give the guests paper streamers to throw.

Menu
Plan a varied menu of sweet and savoury food (pages 54–71) and tie it in to a theme. Keep the portions small. Try open sandwiches, a porcupine or dinosaur made from a chunky dip and vegetable sticks, picture pizzas, crisps, mini sausages, iced cupcakes, fruit fools, dinosaur cake (dragon cake decorated with spots instead of scales), ruby fruit punch, or strawberry shakes.

Toys
Arrange a quiet corner with books and jigsaw puzzles for shy guests who prefer not to join in the games.

I'm a Little Teapot
Four-year-olds still enjoy action songs (page 39).

Dragon cake
Children love dragons and
monsters, so make a cake to
suit their tastes (page 64).

Picture pizzas
Make these exciting
with toppings and
garnishes (page 57).

Warming-up activities

Four-year-olds enjoy making things,
so prepare some craft activities
to break the ice when the
children arrive
(page 47). Make
masks and hats
(pages 32–33)
and provide felt
pens and sticky shapes so that the
children can decorate them. Draw a
bold mural on a sheet of lining paper
for the guests to colour in together.

Games

At this age, children are enthusiastic
about games. Explain the rules slowly
and be prepared to help. Plan up to
eight games (pages 39–50) to last five
minutes each. Avoid competitive
games; play ones that are just fun or
where everyone wins a treat. Adapt
games to a theme by renaming them
and using suitable props. Choose
from Feed the Lion, Monkey's Tail,
Musical Statues, Guess the Sound,
Feely Bag, Balloon Race, Who Has
the Key, Skittles, Freeze Tag, Duck,
Duck, Goose, or the Parachute Game.

Prizes and treats

Put tiny wrapped treats (hooters,
pencils, novelty erasers, bubble
mixture, soap shapes) in a basket
and ask the birthday child to hand
them out as prizes. For going home,
write the guests' names on small
presents (sticker books, small plastic
toys, etc.), hide them, and have a
treasure hunt as the last game.

Four-year-old
Games are
played with
energy and
enthusiasm
at this age.

PARTY PLAN

◊ Children arrive.

◊ Birthday child opens the
presents.

◊ Children decorate party hats,
masks, or mural, or do other
craft activities.

◊ Play two or three games.

◊ Party meal. Take photographs
or shoot a video.

◊ Play four or five more
games.

  ◊ Play Hunt the Present for
going-home presents.

◊ Going-home time.

PARTY TIPS

◊ Prepare a few more games
than you think you will need,
just in case the children race
through them.

◊ Give your helpers a list of
the games. Tell them where the
props are and how to work the
cassette player.

◊ Make sure the birthday child
also gets a treat while he is
handing out prizes.

◊ If the children become too
rowdy, ask them to sit down
and put their hands on their
heads. Wait until they are all
silent, then play a copying
game such as Simon Says.
When they have quietened
down, continue with your
planned programme.

◊ Restrict the treasure hunt
to one room to protect your
furniture and ornaments.

PLANNING A PARTY
— FOR A —
5-YEAR-OLD

A five-year-old child is more grown-up in many ways than a four-year-old. This allows you far more scope in planning a party.

Party polaroids
These make an amusing going-home gift.

Picture roll
Make bread rolls fun for hungry party-goers (page 55).

Birthday pizza
Decorate each pizza with cheese and a ham number "5" (page 57).

Red potion
Mix a colourful cocktail of fruit juices (page 70).

Ice-cream sundae
This strawberry sundae is one of many fruity varieties (page 60).

Fairy-tale cottage cake (page 66)

Guests
Your child may be keen to invite the whole school class to the party. Unless you are hiring a venue and have lots of helpers, restrict the number of guests to no more than ten. Plan a party of 2–2½ hours. Five-year-olds soon wear themselves out and become irritable if expected to behave sociably for longer.

Invitations
Make invitations that tie in with the party theme (pages 28–29) and ask your child to help you make them.

Decorations
With this age group, try more ambitious themes: pirates, wizards and witches, and fairy stories are popular. Decorate the games room, as well as the party table. Your child could help with making streamers (pages 30–31). Hang up balloons decorated with funny faces. If you prepare the materials in advance, the guests can finish off the decorations as a warming-up activity.

Special attractions
Children of this age are beginning to develop their own interests, so you may want to plan something special. Ask all the children to wear fancy dress, or hire an entertainer, or put on a simple magic show. An energetic child would enjoy an outdoor party with races and ballgames, or a visit to the local swimming pool or gym, with a party meal at home afterwards.

Fancy dress
Many five-year-olds really relish a fancy-dress party. Ask them to come to the party in a costume, or provide a box of appropriate clothing for them to put on when they arrive. A hat, cloak, or scarf, and a suitable prop usually do the trick. If any child is reluctant to dress up, tempt them with a small item, such as a stick-on moustache or a headband (page 32). If you know someone who is good at face-painting, invite them to come along and paint the children's faces.

Menu
Many children at this age are hungry after games, but are still picky eaters. The spread should be varied and colourful (pages 54–71). Make picture rolls, mini quiches, picture pizzas, tomato treats, party pretzels, chocolate crispies, fruit kebabs, ice-cream sundaes, birthday cake, real lemonade or sunset punch.

Hide the cake until the party so that it is a surprise for the birthday child as well as for everyone else.

Race Track Game (page 45)

Wizard's costume
Decorate a conical hat (page 33) and a cape with silver moons and stars.

Plate mask
This lion face is easy to make (page 32).

Games

...mes will be the high spot of the ...rty. Plan 10–12, with a variety of ...iet and energetic games, team ...mes, and memory games or brain-...asers (pages 40–50). Make it easier ...r yourself by choosing a few games ...at don't need props. No game ...ould last longer ...an 7–10 ...inutes, or ...redom may ...t in. Try ...ed the Lion, ...ss the ...rcel, Hot ...otato, Musical ...atues, Feely ...g, Guess ...hat?, Memory ...me, Balloon Race, ...easure Hunt, Freeze Tag, ...ck, Duck, Goose, ...rachute Game, or ...essing-up Race.

Prizes and treats

...r a fancy-dress party, wrap ...face paints, false noses, or ...astic jewellery. Put small ...eme-linked toys, such as ...asers, pencils, or stickers, in ...prize chest (page 35) for ...ests to have a lucky dip ...fore they go home. Give ...ch guest a polaroid of ...m- or herself taken at ...e party, and a small ...ce of the party cake ...apped in a napkin.

Five-year-old
A child of this age will look forward to a party for weeks in advance.

PARTY PLAN

◇ Children arrive and birthday child opens presents.

◇ Children dress up or have their faces painted. Take polaroid photographs.

◇ Children finish decorations.

◇ Play three or four games.

◇ Party meal. Take the photographs or film.

◇ Magic show, entertainer, or other special activity, if any.

◇ Play four or six more games.

◇ Lucky dip.

◇ Going-home time.

PARTY TIPS

◇ Put out all the props for the first activity in advance.

◇ Clear as much furniture as you can from the games room.

◇ Be vigilant with the games. Team games are still difficult at this age. You may have to act as a tactful referee and intercept if tempers start to fray.

◇ Keep the momentum of the party going and avoid slow spots between the games, activities, and the party meal.

◇ Keep an eye on bossy or dominant guests and don't allow them to take over the games. If they persist, suggest that they help you out with refereeing the games.

◇ Remember to let the birthday child start off as many games as possible.

PLANNING A PARTY
— FOR —
MIXED AGES

If the children are not all of the same age, plan the party to suit the age of the majority, but make concessions for younger or older children.

Party medal
A child will be proud to wear this (page 35).

Cupcake
This cat face (page 59) has great appeal.

Party bag
Give a similar bag (page 35) to each child, but vary the contents according to age.

Party meal

Unless you have a very large table, it is a good idea to have a separate, smaller table and chairs for younger children at a party. That way they are less likely to be pushed or jostled by the bigger children and you can serve them with a few special titbits to suit their smaller appetites. Instead of cups or beakers, give them cartons of juice with straws to drink.

Seat older children together at one end of the table. Provide one special dish, like mini quiches (page 57), just for them.

Games

Many of the games on pages 38–50 are suitable for most young children, as long as you help the smaller ones. Very young children cannot cope with memory games or brain-teasers, so provide a quiet toy corner for them to play in while the

older guests are playing the more demanding games. Ask your helpers to look after the younger guests if you are too busy.

Older children can easily become bored at a party for toddlers, but they often like helping. Ask them to help you with the cassette player or with refereeing and judging any games. Another option is to set up an activities corner where they can make things like hats (page 47).

Prizes and treats

Make two prize chests (page 35), each with treats suitable for one age group. For going home, treat all the children the same by giving individually named party bags or baskets (pages 34–35) and tailoring the contents to the guest's age.

Mixed ages
Most young children play together happily, but need a little tactful supervision!

Wibbly wobbly game
Older children enjoy this game (page 48) as much as younger ones.

TROUBLESHOOTING

Even the best-planned party can have hiccups. Young children are emotional and easily become over-excited or tearful. Here are suggestions on how to deal with common situations.

Sweets
Don't give out
too many.

**Summer
lolly** (page 60)

Your child's role

A birthday child can easily build up false expectations of what is going to happen at the party. He or she may expect to win every game or to tell everyone what to do. Run through your party plan with your child beforehand and make him feel special by allowing him to start as many games as possible.

Guest refuses to stay

Be accommodating and reassure the child that the parent can stay. Encourage the child by telling him about the special activities or treats that lie in store.

A brother or sister is upset

Brothers and sisters are often quite jealous of a birthday child. Explain to them that they will be the focus of attention on *their* birthday, when it will be their turn to have the party and all the presents. You could give them their own special party task, such as helping you with the props for games, or passing around food at the table.

Child does not join in

Try gentle encouragement, but don't persist. Suggest the child plays with toys or looks at books. If the child is totally uncooperative, leave them alone, but check up on him or her from time to time.

Over-excited and rowdy guests

Play a quiet game such as Sleeping Lions (page 40), which requires no extra props, or read the children a story. Brain-teasers such as the Memory Game (page 45) demand some quiet concentration. With all parties for older children, it is a good idea to make some rooms out-of-bounds and to discourage any running around upstairs.

Child not winning prizes

The best way to avoid this is not to have competitive games at all. Adapt the rules of games (pages 38–50) wherever possible so that there is no one overall winner. Reward as many guests as possible with praise, sweets, or small treats. Alternatively, you can manipulate

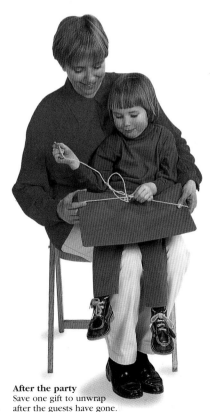

After the party
Save one gift to unwrap
after the guests have gone.

the games to ensure that each child wins in turn; this is easy to do with musical games, where you decide when to stop the music.

Unexpected guests

An extra guest or two sometimes turns up at a party; usually the child is a guest's sibling. To avoid tears and tantrums, make sure that you have extra party plates and cups available, and prepare a few additional treats and party bags (page 35) to keep in reserve.

Rain at an outdoor party

When planning an outdoor party, always have a rainy-day plan up your sleeve. Have an indoor picnic by clearing a space and spreading a cloth on the floor. Some outdoor games (pages 48–50) can be adapted for play inside, but make sure you prepare some indoor games as a contingency measure.

Minor accidents

If a child is hurt during the rough-and-tumble of the party, apply first aid as described on pages 72–78. To avoid injury, clear away the debris of any breakages at once.

Winding down

When all the guests have left, the birthday child may feel a bit forlorn. Instead of rushing to clear up, sit down with your child and look at the presents, read one of the birthday books, or try out one of the new games together. If you have an only child, ask one best friend to stay and play for a little while. Then it is bath, bed, and story time.

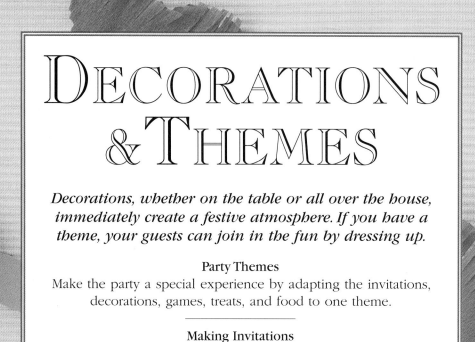

DECORATIONS & THEMES

Decorations, whether on the table or all over the house, immediately create a festive atmosphere. If you have a theme, your guests can join in the fun by dressing up.

Party Themes
Make the party a special experience by adapting the invitations, decorations, games, treats, and food to one theme.

Making Invitations
Announce your party with these novel, hand-crafted invitations to get your guests in a party mood.

Making Decorations
These ideas for colourful streamers, paper chains, pom-poms, balloons, and mobiles can be adapted to fit any party theme.

Making Masks & Hats
Lots of great hats and masks can all be adapted from a few basic designs for a fancy-dress party or a craft activity.

Treats & Prizes
Here is a wealth of suggestions for choosing, wrapping, and presenting party prizes and going-home treats.

TIPS FOR DECORATIONS & THEMES

◇ Decide well in advance whether you will have a party theme or a special feature for the party, so that you can plan accordingly.

◇ Party themes are great fun for children of three years and older, but don't feel obliged to have one. The party can be a success without one.

◇ If your child is going through a craze for a particular idea, such as pirates, plan a theme around it.

◇ Choose envelopes before making your invitations, and cut out the invitations to fit the envelopes.

◇ On each invitation, give the date and venue of the party, the start and collection times, and a phone number for the RSVP. State if the party has a theme or is fancy dress.

◇ Put a footnote on the invitations asking the parents to notify you if any child has an allergy or condition such as asthma, or is a vegetarian.

◇ If short of time, photocopy the invitation and ask your child to help colour them in.

◇ If you don't have much time or money, concentrate on decorating the table and hang up lots of balloons, or just make one huge decoration, such as a party mobile.

◇ Before making the decorations, stock up with useful materials, such as coloured card and foil, crêpe and tissue paper, glue, sticky tape, gummed shapes, and glitter.

◇ Set aside an afternoon with your children for gluing and pasting.

◇ Draw up a shopping list for the prizes and treats. Buying small items such as erasers or party hooters in packs is less costly.

◇ To make sure that you have enough items, sort the prizes into order of play and buy or make party bags and fill them well in advance.

◇ Prepare a surplus of prizes and going-home treats and keep them to hand for unexpected guests.

◇ Make the table look festive with a colourful tablecloth and paper party plates, cups, name cards, and novelty drinking straws. These are often available from supermarkets.

COLOURS & SHAPES

Knowledge of colour and pattern is an important part of early learning, so this theme is ideal for the younger age group.

Coloured paper
Follow a colour theme with bright sweet wrappings and crêpe streamers (page 30).

Party mobile
Make one (page 31) with coloured streamers.

Concertina invitation
Choose a simple shape in the party colours (page 28).

Creating the theme
This is the simplest and the most flexible of themes. Choose any colour or pattern, or a combination, and make all the decorations in the same hues and shapes. Start with your child's favourite colour, or the child's initial, for instance "P" is for Polly and purple. Shapes such as spots, hearts, or stripes are good bases for a theme. Your child could help by colouring in the invitations. Ask the guests to wear clothes in the theme patterns or colours, and get them to decorate coloured headbands (pages 32 & 47).

Games, prizes, and food
Wrap parcels for games in the party colour or pattern, and give prizes such as soap shapes or finger paints. Play colour-match games or change game titles to suit, such as Feed the Spotty Dog (page 40). A few colours like blue are not ideal for food, but with inventive icing, most patterns and combinations of colours are possible.

Streamer hat
Assemble a simple costume with clothes in the party colours and finish off with a hat (page 32).

Prizes and treats
Wrap going-home treats in the party colours (page 35).

Party table
Dress up the table with a paper tablecloth, cups and plates, and party straws in bold colours.

Cut-out invitation
Make this (page 28) in the number shape of the child's age.

RAINBOWS

For this party, choose a combination of several colours and stripes. If the weather is fine, you could have a rainbow party outdoors.

Multi-coloured T-shirt
Children's clothes in rainbow stripes are easy to find.

Cupcakes
Different-coloured icing toppings create a rainbow on a plate.

Paper baskets
A rainbow of colours makes gifts exciting (page 34).

Creating the theme

Base the colours of the party on the seven colours of the rainbow (red, orange, yellow, green, blue, indigo, and violet) and use stripes as much as possible. Make simple folded invitations with the word PARTY outlined on the front, and ask your child to colour in the letters with different-coloured crayons. Invite all the guests to dress in rainbow colours. Make a rainbow cut-out for your front door and hang groups of different coloured balloons from the ceiling, or from tree branches in the garden.

Games, prizes, and food

Break the ice at the start of the party with a mural (page 49) for the children to fill in with multi-coloured crayons or stickers. Use gaily coloured toys and sweets for prizes and wrap each games prop in a different colour. For outdoor games, make rainbow skittles (page 48), or provide striped clothes for a Dressing-up Race (page 50). Make pizzas or quiches (page 57) with "striped" toppings and decorate cupcakes with glacé icing rainbows (page 59).

Rainbow stationery
Give out as prizes gummed paper shapes, paints, and crayons in bright colours.

Pom-poms
Make these to add to the decorations (page 30).

Costume
Ribbons on a cloak and a rainbow mask (page 32) make a jolly outfit.

TEDDY BEARS

Young children will love to have a party at which they and their friends are surrounded by their favourite teddy bears.

Teddy hats
Buy or make a paper cone hat (page 33) for each guest bear.

Cupcake
Make a bear face with glacé icing and chocolate buttons (page 59).

Teddy bear cake
This novelty cake (page 64) will be the highlight of the teddy bears' picnic.

Creating the theme

If young guests bring along their teddy bears, there will be plenty of opportunities for play with the toy "guests". Create the right look with concertina streamers (page 30) in a teddy design and a large cut-out bear for the front door. Encourage the children to join in the fun with headbands (page 32) decorated with teddy ears or bear patterns.

Place your child's teddy bears around the party room and set up a play corner with teddy-bear puzzles and story books. If your child has a tape featuring teddy-bear songs, play this as the guests arrive.

Games, prizes, and food

Choose games that you can adapt to the theme, such as Stick the Nose on the Teddy (page 41). Buy prizes that are decorated with bears and make "picnic baskets" for the going-home treats (page 34). Make teddy-shaped biscuits (page 58), and don't forget the honey!

Mystery parcels
Include teddy-shaped treats in this game (page 44).

Concertina invitation
Announce the party theme with bear-shaped invitations (page 28).

Bear mask
Stick this plate mask (page 32) on a stick to make it easy to hold.

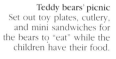

Teddy bears' picnic
Set out toy plates, cutlery, and mini sandwiches for the bears to "eat" while the children have their food.

ANIMALS

Parties with this theme can be adapted to suit any age group. Choose animals from the farmyard, jungle, or cartoons.

Cut-out invitation
Make a different animal for each guest and put them together to make a zoo.

Cut-out invitation
Decorate an animal shape with coloured paper and crayons for a charming invitation (page 28).

Picture biscuit
Decorate a short-bread butterfly with icing and coloured sweets (page 58).

Picture biscuit
This pig is made from chocolate shortbread (page 58).

Creating the theme

Animal characters are some of the most familiar personalities in a young child's world. Buy or make animal party decorations (pages 30–31) and make your own cut-outs to decorate walls and doors.

As an alternative to a teddy-bear party, ask children to bring their favourite stuffed toy animal with them. You could draw animal-face badges to cut out on dressing-up invitations (page 29). For older children, prepare headbands and different animal ears (page 32) and supply crayons so that each guest can colour in a set of ears when they arrive at the party.

Games, prizes, and food

As well as the animal games on pages 40–41, adapt games by changing the titles or verses. Treats can be animal toys, animal stickers, soaps, or erasers. Call the meal "feeding time" and feed "animal" guests with wiggly cheesy shapes (page 57) or "worms".

Animal mask
Try out these ideas (page 32) for an animal disguise.

Picture rolls and party drinks
Transform rolls (page 55) into rabbits or dogs and put animal straws in the drinks.

Costumes
Each child wears clothes in colours that suggest their chosen animal.

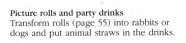

PIRATES

Pirates are familiar characters from adventure stories and provide a wealth of dramatic motifs for older children's parties.

Creating the theme

Dressing-up invitations (page 29) are ideal for a pirate party – you could send guests a cut-out moustache, eye patch, or even buckles for their shoes. Ask the children to wear a basic outfit of shorts and a striped top. Other accessories such as hats and cutlasses can be made or bought.

Black, gold, silver, and red are good colours for this theme. Use skull-and-crossbones cut-outs around the house; pin one to the front door, stick one on a window, and hang a party mobile over the table or in the games room.

Games, prizes, and food

Adapt Stick the Tail on the Donkey (page 41) by drawing a map of a desert island so that the children can guess the position of the buried treasure. Play Who Has the Key to the Treasure Chest? (page 47), and so on. Make a treasure chest (page 35) as a lucky dip for going-home treats. Give food a nautical look with small flags, edible garnishes, and icing, and call the drinks "grog".

Headgear
Provide pirate hats and send invitations with cut-out eye patches (page 29).

Swashbuckler
Shorts, a striped T-shirt, and a buckle, cutlass, and hat make a fun costume.

Party mobil
Decorate this (pag 31) with blac ribbon and cu out anchor and cutlasse

Pirate booty
Small items like these chocolate coins and parrot soap make good prizes.

Hearty fare
Make these edible ships (page 54) for a piratical spread.

Novelty brew
Serve drinks (pages 70–71) with a skull-and-crossbones on each straw.

FAIRY TALES

Traditional themes of knights, dragons, and fairies spark children's imaginations and take on a new lease of life at a party.

Toy jewellery
Use as prizes bracelets that look like gems.

Headband
Add a star for a fairy princess (page 32).

Creating the theme

Choose one particular fairy tale or use a range of ideas and characters from children's legends. If they are given a few props, children love the chance to act out their favourite stories. Send dressing-up invitations with, for instance, stars for the guests to make into fairy headbands or wands. Reinforce the theme with the decorations, in pink, gold, and silver for fairies, or green and purple to echo a knight's heraldic colours. Put up fairy lights and swags of white net on walls to create a fairy palace, or hang up streamers (page 30) and mobiles (page 31) to suggest court pennants.

Games, prizes, and food

Wave a wand before an answer is revealed to turn mystery games into magic tricks. Look for Cinderella's slipper in the Treasure Hunt (page 46). Choose prizes such as fairy jewels, star stickers, plastic trolls, monsters, frogs, and sugar mice. Serve cheese wands (page 57) and "fairy" fruit punch (page 70), and make a fairy-tale cottage cake (page 66) as a table centre-piece.

Party bag
Give as a going-home treat (page 35).

Knight's helmet
Make this helmet from coloured card and crêpe paper.

Open sandwiches
Cut these in the shape of stars, butterflies, and flowers (page 54).

Courtly potion
Dress up drinks (page 70) with heraldic straws.

Fairy wand
Use a star from a dressing-up invitation (page 29) for a fairy wand.

Dragon cake
Defeat the dragon by eating him (page 64).

WITCHES & WIZARDS

Scary things hold a fascination for many young children, so a spooky party with its mix of fun and fantasy will have just the right appeal.

Hallowe'en balloons
Decorate balloons with pumpkin cut-outs or cat faces and hang them up.

⚠ **CAUTION!**
Balloons can be a choking hazard.

Magician's hat
Decorate a conical card hat (page 33) with silver stars and moons.

Creating the theme

Autumn or winter is a good time of year for a spooky party. Costumes are easy to create: a ghost needs just a piece of old sheet with eye-, mouth-, and armholes cut in it. For a wizard, make a cloak from a rectangle of dark fabric with ribbon ties stitched on. Paint silver cobwebs on a black cloak for a witch. To make a magic wand, roll up a sheet of dark blue paper diagonally into a narrow pointed tube. Tape the edges and add star and moon stickers. Make strings of moons and stars (page 31) to hang near the party table. To light the table, hollow out a pumpkin and put a torch inside.

Games, prizes, and food

Use ghostly sounds like a miaow or creaking door to play games such as Guess the Sounds (page 44). Fill a Feely Bag (page 44) with plastic insects and "witches' hair" (cold spaghetti). Creepy-crawly toys make good prizes. Call drinks "magic brews" and serve with black grapes, moon-shaped pastry bites (page 57), and ice cream with red berry sauce "blood" (page 60).

Window mobiles
Cut shapes from thin card and suspend them on thin silver ribbon.

Witches' food
Make a feast with web-patterned cupcakes (page 59) and Red Potion (page 70).

Wizard's hat cake
This decorated sponge cake is simple to make (page 68).

Creepy treats
Buy spider-shaped erasers and pencil sharpeners.

Witch's outfit
All you need is a hat (page 33), broom, and cobwebby cloak.

KINGS & QUEENS

Children's rhymes and legends provide a multitude of traditional regal characters that children can impersonate by dressing up and role-playing.

Regal hats
Supply guests with crowns (page 32) and princess's hats (page 33).

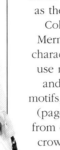

Creating the theme

Invite children to come to the party as the Queen of Hearts, Old King Cole, the King of the Sea, the Mermaid Princess, or other royal characters. To create a regal effect, use rich colours like red, purple, and gold, together with crown motifs, for cut-outs or party mobiles (page 31). "Jewels" can be made from coloured foil and stuck on to crowns or caskets. Purple or red lining material makes a silky robe that can be edged with "ermine" made from cotton wool and black paper spots. Prepare gold-coloured card shoe buckles for guests to decorate with coloured felt or foil when they arrive.

Games, prizes, and food

Adapt game names and play Royal (Musical) Statues (page 43) and The Queen's (Mr Bear's) Footsteps (page 41). Hand out riches such as "gold" coins or "jewelled" hairslides as prizes. Hold a "banquet" with golden or silver tableware; serve open sandwiches (page 54) and pastry bites (page 57) in coronet shapes.

Crown headband
Decorate the crown (page 32) with coloured foil to suggest precious jewels.

Royal coffer
Decorate a prize box (page 35) and fill with treats like these coloured foil stickers.

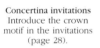

Concertina invitations
Introduce the crown motif in the invitations (page 28).

Royal drinks
Decorate straws with paper coronets.

Fruit kebabs
These kebabs (page 60) look like rich beads.

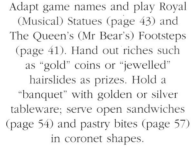

Picture pizza
Cheese stars and sweet pepper pieces make the pizza (page 57) look like a royal emblem.

Regal robes
Simple capes can look like flowing robes.

MAKING INVITATIONS

It can be just as much fun to give as well as receive an original party invitation like the ones below. Take a little time to enjoy designing and decorating invitations with the help of your child.

CONCERTINA INVITATIONS

You will need

Paper; scissors; pencil; non-toxic glue and thin coloured card (optional)

These folded invitations are simple to make. Your child may recognize the technique from nursery school artwork.

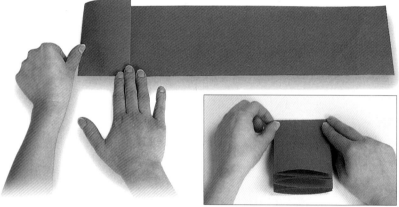

1 Cut out a 50 x 8cm (20 x 3in) paper strip. Make a fold 7cm (2⅛in) from one end, and press it down. Fold the paper back on itself. Repeat until the entire strip is pleated.

2 Draw your design on the top fold of paper, making sure that the design touches the edges of the folded paper at several points. For a clown, leave the hands and feet touching.

3 Cut around the design, preserving the joins along the pleats. Open out the paper concertina. You can write straight onto the concertina, or glue one end to a folded card.

CUT-OUT INVITATIONS

You will need

Coloured paper or card; scissors; pens, glitter, or cotton wool for decoration

Area left blank for the guest's name and the party details

Cotton-wool tail

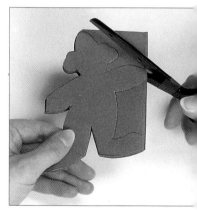

Cut out bold shapes of animals or toys from coloured paper or card. Decorate each cut-out with coloured paper pieces and remember to leave space in which to write the invitatio

DRESSING-UP INVITATIONS

You will need

Thin coloured card; scissors; pens; non-toxic glue; glitter

courage your guests to dress up by nding them invitations that double as fancy-dress cut-out accessories. aw the outline of the accessory on iece of card and write the wording ound it. You could draw a mask age 32), a fairy star, or a pirate eye tch, according to the party theme.

Star attached to a headband (page 32) for a fairy princess

Pirate props
Draw an eye patch and a bushy moustache for guests to cut out and wear.

Cut-out eye patch is threaded with elastic

iry star
is glitter star could be ed to a short stick to ıke a fairy wand.

INVITATION CARDS

There are several ways of making simple card invitations that look unusual and colourful. Use a computer printout or a colour photocopy of the birthday child's own design, or personalize the wording.

Techno invitations
Use your home computer to print out a design based on your child's drawing; paste it onto thin card. The child could also colour in a photocopy of his own drawing.

Personalized invitations
Make invitations unique by linking each guest's name to the design, e.g. send this card to "Lucy Duck", "Tom Duck", and so on.

Collage of torn tissue paper

MAKING DECORATIONS

Brighten up the party room and create a festive atmosphere with paper chains, streamers, and pom-poms. The decorations are easy to make and your child will enjoy helping you.

PAPER CHAIN

You will need

Different-coloured paper or crêpe paper; ruler; pencil; scissors; non-toxic glue

1 Cut the different-coloured papers into 2.5 x 18cm (1 x 7in) strips.
2 Glue together the ends of one strip to form a ring. Loop a strip through the ring and glue.
3 Continue adding new loops until the chain is the desired length.

CREPE STREAMER

You will need

Different-coloured crêpe paper; scissors; sticky tape

1 Cut a strip of equal width from two different packs of folded crêpe paper.
2 Snip along the edges of each strip to make a fringe.
3 Tape the two strips together at one end and twist all the way along to form a spiral. Hang up the streamer immediately to keep the spiral intact.

CONCERTINA STREAME

You will need

Coloured paper strip 50 x 8cm (20 x 3in); ruler; pencil; scissors

1 Pleat the entire strip of paper by folding it forwards and then backwards every 7cm (2½in).
2 Draw a shape on the top pleat, making sure that part of the drawin touches the folds on both sides.
3 Cut around the shape, preserving the folds, and open out the streame

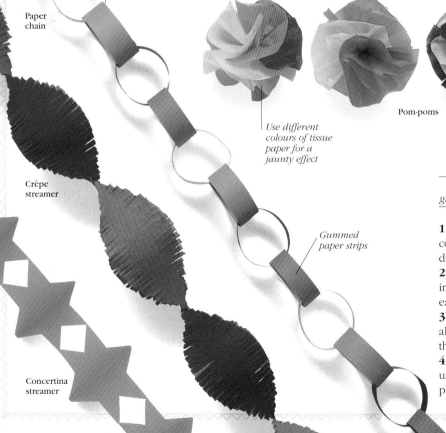

Paper chain

Crêpe streamer

Concertina streamer

Pom-poms

Use different colours of tissue paper for a jaunty effect

Gummed paper strips

POM-POMS

You will need

Folded coloured tissue paper; cup o glass; pencil; scissors; needle and thre

1 Draw eight circles on two or thre colours of folded tissue paper by drawing around a cup or glass.
2 Cut out the circles and fold them into quarters. Thread the point of each quarter onto a knotted thread.
3 Make two small stitches to fasten all the points together and cut the thread, leaving some thread hangin
4 Open out each circle of paper an use the loose thread to hang up the pom-pom. Repeat for each pom-po

String streamer

STRING STREAMER

You will need

Scissors; ribbon; darning needle; cut-out coloured card shapes; string

1 Thread the end of a piece of ribbon through the top of each card shape, and knot it securely.

2 Trim the string to the required length of your streamer.
3 Attach the card shapes to the string by tying their ribbons at evenly spaced intervals along the streamer.

——— Variation ———

Substitute streamers or strips of crêpe paper for the card shapes.

ty mobile

PARTY MOBILE

You will need

Cut-out coloured card shapes; ribbon; scissors; darning needle; hula or wire hoop; tinsel or crêpe paper; string

Prepare the shapes as for a string streamer (see above).
Bind the hoop with tinsel or strips of crêpe paper.
Cut four 45cm (18in) lengths of string. Tie one end of ch length to the hoop. Knot the other ends at the top.
Bind the string with tinsel or ribbon. Tie on the shapes.

PARTY BALLOONS

Decorate balloons with gummed paper and put them high up where children cannot reach. Young children can choke on bits of a burst balloon or on a deflated balloon, so always supervise children playing with balloons and clear away any debris immediately.

⚠ CAUTION!
Balloons can be a choking hazard.

MAKING MASKS & HATS

*For a fancy-dress or theme party, use simple materials such as
card, ribbons, or crêpe paper to create masks and hats that enable
children to act out their favourite fairy stories.*

PLATE MASKS

You will need

*Paper plates; scraps of coloured
paper or card; felt pens; non-toxic
glue; scissors; straws or short sticks*

1 To make faces of animals or
fairy-tale characters, decorate each
paper plate with a textured collage
of coloured paper shapes.
2 Alternatively, draw a face in the
centre of each plate with felt pens.
3 Glue a straw or stick to the plate
so that the mask can be held up.

Bear mask   Lion mask   Rabbit mask

CUT-OUT MASKS

You will need

*Thin coloured card; scissors; narrow
elastic; coloured paper or glitter*

Rainbow mask

Butterfly mask

1 Cut the card into a mask shape.
2 Cut holes for the eyes and elastic.
3 Decorate the mask with paper or
glitter, and attach elastic to the sides.

PARTY HEADBAND

You will need

*Thin coloured card; scissors; sticky tape;
non-toxic glue or double-sided tape*

1 Cut out a strip of card, about
5cm (2in) wide, to fit your child's
head, and tape the ends together.
2 Stick on decorative shapes or
ears (see animal headband, right).
3 For a crown, cut deep zig-zags
into a 13cm (5in) wide headband.

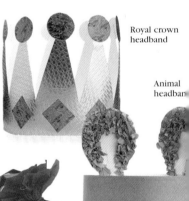

Royal crown headband

Animal headband

Streamer hat
*To make this
jolly hat, cut a strip
of crêpe paper 30 x 60cm
(12 x 24in). Fold the short
edge inside a headband
(see left), and glue it
down. Gather the paper
at the top and tie it with
crêpe streamers.*

MAKING A CONICAL HAT

You will need

...ring; thin card; pencil; scissors; sticky
tape; narrow elastic (optional)

...nical hats are easy to make and
...n be used as simple party hats for
...ests. Adapt the basic conical hat to
...ke wizard, clown, or princess hats
... theme parties (see below). Use
...stic, if needed, to keep the hat on.
...asure your child's head with a
...ce of string before making the hat.

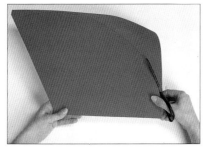

1 Use the measuring string to mark
out the curved edge of a fan shape
on card. Trace the curve of the string
with a pencil. Cut out the fan shape.

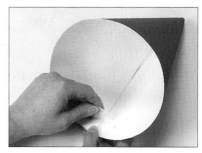

2 To make a cone, tape down the
straight ends on the inside. If
desired, make small holes on two
sides and thread elastic through.

MAKING A BRIMMED HAT

You will need

Conical hat (see above); thin card;
pencil; scissors; sticky tape

Adding a simple brim to a conical hat
can enhance a fancy-dress costume.
You can decorate the brim with
stickers or pieces of cut-out card to
reflect the theme of the party.

Silver brim
enlivens
purple hat

1 Stand the conical hat on a sheet
of card and draw around the base.
...raw a circle 8cm (3in) farther out
...d another 2.5cm (1in) farther in.
...t along the inner and outer circles.

2 Snip at short intervals around
the inner circle to the depth of
the middle circle, making a fringe.
Carefully bend up the fringed edge
so that it fits inside the conical hat.

3 Tape the fringed edge to the
hat base to make a brim.
For a jazzy finish, decorate
the brim with card of a
contrasting hue.

HAT VARIATIONS

A hat is the crowning glory of a fancy-dress costume. You can easily
adapt conical hats to suit a variety of characters by adding a brim or
streamers, and decorating the hat with stickers, paints, or coloured paper.

Princess's hat
Attach coloured streamers or
strips of crêpe paper to the top
of a conical hat to make a
medieval royal headdress.

Witch's hat
Make a conical brimmed hat in
black card. Draw silver cobwebs
and stick on gold-paper spiders
to achieve a spooky look.

TREATS & PRIZES

Children love to receive treats and prizes at a party. Choose items that relate to the theme of the party and make sure that they are shared out equally.

PAPER BASKET

Make a basket for each child. They can use it to hold any prizes they win or you can fill it with treats for them.

You will need

Thick coloured paper 23cm (9in) square; scissors; sticky tape; thin card

1 Fold the paper in half four times. Unfold it to see the paper divided into 16 squares. Cut once along the fold of each corner to the first crease.

2 Fold two adjacent sides upwards along the first crease. Tape the corner square of one side securely behind the other side, as shown.

3 Fold up the third side and tape the corner as before. Fold up the last side and tape both the corners. Make sure all the corners are secure.

4 Cut out a 25 x 2.5cm (10 x 1in) strip of thin card for a handle. Tape the ends to opposite sides of the basket. Decorate the basket.

Going-home gift
Make a basket and fill it with treats for each child to take home as a party souvenir.

Paper baskets

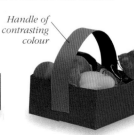

Handle of contrasting colour

PARTY BAGS

You will need

Coloured card or strong tissue paper; scissors; coloured sticky tape; ribbon

For a tall bag, cut out a 38 x 13cm (15 x 5in) rectangle of card. Fold in half and tape the sides together. Tape a short length of ribbon to the top. For a round bag, cut out four 35cm (14in) tissue squares. Put treats in the middle, gather up, and tie with ribbon.

Tall bag   Round bags

PARTY MEDALS

You will need

Large chocolate bars and cake cases or round chocolate biscuits; gold or silver foil; 70cm (28in) narrow ribbons

These medals are simple to make and are ideal prizes for party games. Use round chocolate biscuits or make the medal shapes yourself. Do this by pouring about 0.5cm (⅛in) of melted chocolate into each cake case and leaving them in the fridge to set.

1 Wrap the chocolate biscuit or chocolate shape in a 13cm (5in) square of foil. Smooth it down. Lay the medal on the centre of the ribbon.

2 Bring the ribbon around the medal and tie a firm knot at the top of the medal. Tie another knot where the ribbon ends meet.

Party medal
The child can either keep it or eat it.

PRIZE CHEST

Prize chest

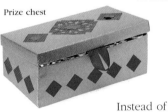

Instead of individual party bags, you could make a "lucky dip" or prize chest. Cover a medium-sized box and lid with coloured paper and decorate to reflect the party theme. Attach the lid to the box with coloured tape hinges. Line with tissue paper. Fill the chest with wrapped gifts such as crayons, sweets, or plastic toys. Each child has a turn at picking out a prize. Put fancy-dress items in the chest to match the theme.

When choosing treats to fill a chest, or party baskets or bags, ensure that they suit the children's age group (pages 8–15).

Sweets

Springy frog   Toy car

Wax crayons

Hooter

PARTY GAMES

Games are the high spot of the party for many children and there is a huge variety to choose from. Plan a selection of suitable games well in advance.

Songs & Rhymes
Simple singing and action games based on nursery rhymes.

Musical Games
Energetic old favourites requiring only a few basic props.

Brain-teasers
Easy guessing or memory games for young children.

Action Games
Team and group games, as well as craft activities.

Outdoor Games
Ball games, races, and outdoor activities.

Entertainers
How to choose and book a children's entertainer.

PARTY GAMES TIPS

◊ Read through this chapter and choose a variety and number of games suitable for your child's age group (see also pages 8–15). Make a list of your chosen games and props.

◊ Always plan more games than you think you need; it is hard to anticipate how long games will take, as some will be more successful than others.

◊ Avoid competitive games, as most young children cannot cope with losing. Plan some games with no winners and others where several or all the children win little treats.

◊ Write out the order of play. Start with a warming-up game or activity, alternate the quiet and energetic games, and end on a quiet game.

◊ In case bad weather affects an outdoor party, plan a few indoor games to keep in reserve. Some outdoor games can be played indoors, if necessary.

◊ Let the birthday child feel special by starting each game or by choosing the first player.

◊ Adapt the names of games to fit your party theme and choose appropriate props and prizes.

◊ Prepare everything you need in the right order so that the games follow one another smoothly, without a lull.

◊ An adult helper is vital for games. They can help supervise, operate the cassette player, or watch for trouble.

◊ Before starting a game, explain the rules slowly and clearly and make sure every child knows what to do.

◊ Avoid games where only one child at a time plays, or where too many children are "out". Let these children miss a turn, then join in again, or involve them in another activity.

◊ Children have a short attention span, so play each game for 5–10 minutes.

◊ Be flexible. You may need to introduce a quiet game if things are getting rowdy, allow one to run on if it is a wild success, or abandon one that doesn't interest the children.

◊ Prepare to cheat, so that every child has a turn. Be firm but fair with difficult guests.

SONGS & RHYMES

These songs and rhymes are especially good for toddlers and small children, and give shy guests a chance to join in. Go through the songs first, demonstrating the actions, before singing together.

RING-A-RING-A-ROSES
Action song for age 2 upwards

(Join hands and walk around in
a circle as you sing this song)
Ring-a-ring-a-roses,
A pocket full of posies,
A-tishoo, a-tishoo,
We all fall down.
(Everyone falls down on the floor)

(Sit in a circle with hands joined)
Picking up the daisies,
Picking up the daisies,
A-tishoo, a-tishoo,
We all jump up!
(All jump up)

HERE WE GO ROUND THE MULBERRY BUSH
Action song for age 2 upwards

Chorus
(The children hold hands and skip
around in a circle)
Here we go round the mulberry bush,
The mulberry bush, the mulberry bush,
Here we go round the mulberry bush
On a cold and frosty morning.

Verses
(The children copy you as you mime
the actions)
This is the way we wash our hands,
Wash our hands, wash our hands,
This is the way we wash our hands
On a cold and frosty morning.

This is the way we brush our hair,
Brush our hair, brush our hair,
This is the way we brush our hair
On a cold and frosty morning.

Suggested additional verses
This is the way we clean our teeth ...
This is the way we go to school ...
This is the way we eat our tea ...
This is the way we go to sleep ...

Ring-a-ring-a-roses

F YOU'RE HAPPY AND YOU KNOW IT
Action song for age 2 upwards

you're happy and you know it,
ap your hands.
lap, clap)
you're happy and you know it,
ap your hands.
lap, clap)
you're happy and
u know it,
nd you really want
show it,
you're happy and
u know it,
ap your hands.
lap, clap)

uggested additional
rses
ake your head ...
uch your nose ...
in around ...
amp your feet ...
o the twist ...

GRANDMA'S SPECTACLES
Hand rhyme for age 3 upwards

These are Grandma's spectacles.
(Make circles around eyes
with fingers)
This is Grandma's hat.
(Put hands over head)
This is the way she folds
her hands
And puts them in her lap.
(Put hands in lap)

These are Grandad's
spectacles.
(Make circles round eyes)
This is Grandad's hat.
(Put hands over head)
This is the way he folds
his arms,
(Fold arms)
And has a little nap.
(Pretend to doze off)

If you're happy
and you know it

LITTLE BUNNY
Hand rhyme for age 3 upwards

There was a little bunny who lived
in the wood.
He wiggled his ears as a good
bunny should.
(Children put their hands up on each
side of their head and wiggle them)

He hopped like a squirrel,
(Make fingers of one hand hop
up other arm)
He wiggled by a tree,
(Ear-wiggling action)
He hopped by a duck,
(Finger-hopping action)
And he wiggled by me.
(Point finger to chest)

He stared at the squirrel,
(Make circles around eyes
with fingers)
He peeped round the tree,
(Peep through hands)
He stared at the duck,
(Circles around eyes with fingers)
But he winked at me.
(Point finger to chest and wink)

I'M A LITTLE TEAPOT
Action song for age 3 upwards

m a little teapot,
hort and stout.
ere's my handle,
Put hand on hip)
ere's my spout.
Bend other arm up)

hen the brew is ready,
ear me shout,
Tip me up
Bend to the side)
nd pour me out."

I'm a little teapot

ANIMAL GAMES

Young children are fascinated by animal characters, and will especially relish the opportunity to play the part of an animal in some of these activities and games.

Sleeping lions

SLEEPING LIONS
Age 2 upwards

You will need

Small treats for prizes

1 When you call out "Sleeping lions", each child drops onto the floor and lies as still as possible with eyes shut.
2 Give prizes to the most motionless children.

FEED THE LION
Age 3 upwards

You will need

A cardboard box with a lion's face made out of coloured card and decorated with crêpe paper (the lion's mouth should be a large hole)

A skipping rope or piece of string

Balls of newspaper or tissue paper, or soft foam balls

1 Stand the box on a stool or low table, with the lion's open mouth facing outwards.
2 Make a straight line with the skipping rope or string on the floor, a few feet away from the lion.
3 Ask each child, "Can you feed the lion?" The children stand behind the line and take turns to throw the balls into the lion's mouth.
4 After a few minutes, see how much "food" is inside the lion. When the lion is "full", stop the game.

—————— Variation ——————
Give older children three balls each, and see who can toss all three into the lion's mouth.

Feed the lion

POOR CAT
Age 3 upwards

The children sit in a circle and choose someone to be the "cat". The cat prowls around the inside of the circle on all fours and stops in front of one child at a time. The cat must miaow very sadly and try to make the chosen child laugh. If the child stays serious for three miaows, he becomes the cat and tries to make the others laugh.

MR BEAR'S FOOTSTEPS
Age 3 upwards

One child is "Mr Bear" and stands at one end of the room facing a wall. The other children start at the other end of the room and creep quietly towards Mr Bear.
As soon as he hears a sound, Mr Bear turns around. If he sees anyone moving, that child has to go back and start again.
When a child manages to touch Mr Bear, the two children change places and the game starts again.

———— Variation ————
Call the game Grandma's, King's, Pussy Cat's, or Witch's Footsteps.

THE FARMYARD
Age 3 upwards

You need to be a good storyteller for this game. Sit the children in a circle around you.
Give each child the name of a farmyard animal – more than one child can be any particular animal.
Tell the children to make their animal sounds each time their animal is mentioned.
Tell the story of a day at the farm, and mention all the animals in turn.
Encourage the children to be as noisy as they like and keep the story simple and funny.

Stick the tail on the donkey

STICK THE TAIL ON THE DONKEY
Age 4 upwards

You will need

A large picture of a donkey taped to a door or easel
A tail made from card and streamers
Double-sided sticky tape
A blindfold made from a scarf or piece of dark fabric (optional)
A pen or pencil
Bag of small treats

1 Put some sticky tape on the top end of the donkey's tail.
2 Ask the children to line up and ask the first child to close her eyes, or wear a blindfold.
3 Guide her to the picture, turn her around once, and ask her to stick the tail in the right place.
4 Mark the place where the child puts the tail by drawing a cross and writing the child's name next to it. Remove the tail and repeat until everyone has had a go.
5 The winner is the child whose cross is in the most accurate position.
6 Ask the winner, or winners, to pick a prize from a "nosebag" of goodies.

———— Variations ————
◊ Call the game Stick the Nose on the Teddy Bear, Stick the Tail on the Dinosaur, Stick the Hat on the Witch, and so on, according to the theme.
◊ For a pirates' party, draw an island map; the children stick a paper casket where they think treasure is buried.

MONKEY'S TAIL
Age 4 upwards

You will need

A ball of wool
2 empty jars
2 wax crayons
Small treats for prizes

1 Two children at a time take part.
2 Tie a long piece of wool around each child's waist and let the "tail" trail down behind so that it reaches almost to the floor.
3 Tie a crayon on to the end of each tail. Place a large jar on the floor behind each child.
4 Each child has to try to get the crayon into the jar before the other, without using their hands.
5 If there are only a few children, have play-offs between the winners from each pair, until you get "Top Monkey". Give all the winners a prize.

MUSICAL GAMES

All children adore musical games, and they will also happily jig about to music. To play these games, you will need a tape recorder and tapes of nursery rhymes or favourite theme tunes.

PASS THE PARCEL
Age 2 upwards

You will need

A present wrapped in many layers of paper (at least as many layers as there are guests)

A surprise sweet or tiny present in each layer of paper

1 Ask the children to sit in a circle. Play some music and ask the children to pass the parcel around the circle.
2 Stop the music. The child holding the parcel unwraps just one layer of paper to find a small treat inside.
3 Start the music again and encourage the children to pass the parcel. Watch where you stop the music, to ensure that each child has a turn.
4 The game continues until the parcel has been completely unwrapped and the winner gets the last layer with the surprise present inside.

MUSICAL BUMPS
Age 2 upwards

You will need

Small treats (optional)

1 Play a music tape of nursery rhymes or theme tunes and ask the children to jump up and down, or dance, to the music.
2 Every now and then, stop the music. When it stops, the children sit down as fast as they can. Call out the name of the first child to sit down.
3 Young children are happy to carry on like this. For older children, give a prize to the winner of each round. Don't give out any sweets, as a child might choke on them while dancing.

MATCH THE BALLOON
Age 3 upwards

You will need

Different-coloured badges made from card and safety pins

Balloons in different colours

1 Ask the children to sit in a circle and give each one a different-coloured badge. (You can repeat colours as long as there are enough balloons in those colours.)
2 Put the balloons in the middle of the circle of children. There should be the same number of balloons as there are children.
3 While the music plays, the children all walk in a circle around the pile of coloured balloons.
4 When the music stops, call out a colour. The child with that colour badge has to find the matching balloon and hold it up. The game continues until each child has a matching balloon.

⚠ CAUTION
Balloons can be a choking hazard.

Pass the parcel

HOT POTATO
Age 3 upwards

You will need
big "hot potato", such as a beach ball or some other unbreakable object

Ask the children to stand in a circle and give the birthday child the "hot potato" to hold.

Play some music. Ask the birthday child to pass round the hot potato. When you stop the music, the child who is holding the hot potato in her hands has to do a simple forfeit, such as hopping on the spot, turning around, or running round the circle.

Continue the game until every child has performed a forfeit.

Hot potato

MUSICAL STATUES
Age 4 upwards

You will need
Small treats (optional)

1 To start the game, play some music and ask the children to dance, skip, or hop around the room in time to the music.
2 Every now and then, stop the music. As soon as it stops, each child has to "freeze" or stand still. Anyone moving must sit down and miss a go.
3 Start the music again. When the children freeze, you can give small prizes to those who are most "frozen". Don't include sweets as prizes, as a dancing child could choke on them.

— Variation —
Call the game Steady Teddies, Posing Pirates, Wooden Witches, Royal Statues, Frozen Fairies, and so on, according to the party theme.

Musical statues

MAKING MUSIC

Young children in particular will enjoy this activity. Saucepan drums and wooden-spoon drumsticks are easy for them to use.

Children love to make a noise, so give them some simple instruments made from ordinary household objects. Make rattles and shakers by firmly sealing a little dried pasta or a few coloured buttons in sturdy plastic containers. Put on some music with a strong rhythm and encourage the children to play along. After each tune, the children can swap instruments.

Brain-teasers

Challenge the natural curiosity of nursery- and school-age children with these guessing and memory games. Children find the process of deduction both absorbing and exciting.

MYSTERY PARCELS
Age 3 upwards

You will need

6 items with distinctive shapes, wrapped in brightly coloured paper

Notebook and pencil (optional)

Mystery parcel shoe

1 Ask the children to sit in a circle and pass the mystery parcels around, one at a time.
2 Let the children decide as a group what is in each parcel, then unwrap it to see if they are right.
3 For older children, write down individual guesses and announce winners at the end.

Mystery parcel aeroplane

Mystery parcel teddy bear

GUESS THE SOUND
Age 3 upwards

You will need

A screen of some sort

5 or 6 objects that make a distinctive sound, such as a whistle, rattle, bicycle bell, box of crayons, or tape of animal noises and everyday sounds

1 Hide the objects behind the screen.
2 Sit the children down in front of the screen.
3 Make a sound behind the screen with one object and ask the children in turn if they can guess what it is.
4 Ask each child who guesses correctly to come and help you make the next sound.

FEELY BAG
Age 3 upwards

You will need

A pillow case

Balls of screwed-up newspaper

5 objects with distinctive shapes and textures, such as a spoon, watch, apple, dried pasta, and toy car

Small treats for prizes

1 Fill the pillow case with the balls of newspaper and the chosen selection of objects.
2 Hold the pillow case tightly at the top, leaving an opening just big enough for a child to reach inside.
3 Each child in turn feels the object and guesses what they are. Make a note of what they say.
4 At the end, tell the children the answers. Give prizes to the winners.

Feely bag

Race track game

RACE TRACK GAME
Age 4 upwards

You will need

A ramp made from coloured card, or a plank or tray, balanced on a book

A toy car or truck

2 markers, such as crayons or toy figures

1 Two children play at a time. Have a toy car ready at the top of the ramp.
2 Sit the children close to the ramp and ask the first two each to put a marker where they think the car will stop at the bottom.
3 Let the car roll down the ramp and see whose marker is nearest the spot where the car stops.
4 Repeat with two more children, until each child has had a go.

GUESS WHAT?
Age 4 upwards

You will need

Selection of cards, each with a simple word describing an animal, such as CAT, COW, or DOG, written on it

One child leaves the room, and the others are shown a word card. Read out the word, bring in the child, and ask the other children to mime the meaning of the word. The child has three guesses, then someone else takes a turn to leave the room. A new word is chosen, then acted out.

—Variation—
Write a simple action on the cards, such as SIT or JUMP.

MEMORY GAME
Age 4 upwards

You will need

A tray

6 or 7 household objects and toys

1 Show the children the tray with the objects on it for several minutes.
2 Ask them to look carefully and try to remember all the objects.
3 Take the tray away and remove one object, without the children seeing.

4 Show them the tray again. Can they see what's missing?
5 If younger children want to join in the game, ask them to help the older children remember by naming all the objects in turn.

Memory game

ACTION GAMES

These games are just as exciting for the younger children as they are for the older ones. As well as the physical activities, you could involve the children in simple craft projects.

BALLOON RACE
Age 3 upwards

You will need
Lengths of string for the start and finish lines

A balloon for each player

1 Lay out start and finish lines on the party room floor with the string.
2 Divide the children into two teams and give each child a balloon. (All the children in one team could have balloons of the same colour.)
3 Each child in turn has to get from the start to the finish line holding the balloon between his or her knees. If they drop the balloons, they have to go back to the start and try again. You may need to join in at first, to show how it is done!
4 When both teams have completed the course, the game is over.

⚠ **CAUTION!**
Balloons can be a choking hazard.

LITTLE LIMBO
Age 3 upwards

You will need
3 chairs, 2 with rungs

1 broom

1 Place one chair at one end of the room. Put the two with rungs at the other end, with the chairbacks facing each other. Lay the broom across the top of the chairbacks.
2 Line up the children by the single chair. Ask them to follow the birthday child as she goes under the broom, and back to the single chair.
3 Lower the broom on to the chair seats and repeat the procession.
4 Lastly, lower the broom on to the chair rungs and ask the children to crawl under it.

TREASURE HUNT
Age 3 upwards

You will need
Pieces of "treasure", such as large wooden beads, building blocks, sweet chocolate gold coins, or jigsaw piece

1 Hide the treasure around the hou (or room) in places that are not too difficult to find.
2 Ask the children to see how many treats they can find. Watch out for children who don't find anything an drop treasure close to where they ar so that everyone finds something.
3 After a few minutes, stop the sear and count up the trophies or collect together the jigsaw pieces. The children can now eat edible finds or sit down to put the jigsaw togethe

Balloon race

46

WHO HAS THE KEY?

Age 3 upwards

You will need

A loop of string or rope long enough to form a circle that includes all the children

A key

Thread the key onto the string and the ends of the string together. The players have to stand or sit in a circle, holding on to the string with both hands. One player holds the key in his or her hand so that it is hidden from view.

3 One child is chosen to stand or sit in the centre of the circle with his eyes closed.

4 The others pass the key along the string. When the key is hidden, they shout, "Ready!", and the child in the middle opens his eyes.

He then tries to guess which of the other children is holding the key.

5 If he is right, the children swap over; if not, he shuts his eyes and the key is passed around again.

6 Let the child in the circle have three guesses before someone else has a turn.

Who has the key?

THINGS TO MAKE

Creative activities are good for breaking the ice at the beginning of a party, and the children will have something special of their own to take home later. Make the activity as easy as possible and prepare all the materials beforehand. Enlist help from other parents.

Royal crown headband

HEADBAND HATS

Age 3 upwards

You will need

Old newspapers

Card headband strips (page 32)

For decoration: gummed shapes, stickers, coloured paper, sweet wrappers, foil, cotton wool, glitter, non-toxic glue

Double-sided tape

1 Spread sheets of newspaper over a low table or on the floor to create a crafts area and give each child a card headband strip.

2 Let the children decorate the headbands with their chosen materials.

3 When they have finished, measure each child's head and tape the headband to fit.

FUNNY FACES

Age 4 upwards

You will need

Large faces cut out of old colour magazines

Pairs of blunt-ended children's scissors

Non-toxic glue

1 Give a cut-out face and a pair of scissors to each child.

2 Show the children how to cut the faces across into three horizontal strips, so that the eyes, nose, and mouth are each visible in a strip. Help with the cutting-up if needed.

3 The children can mix and match the sections to make funny faces, or they can glue them onto card to take home after the party.

OUTDOOR GAMES

*In fine weather, take the children outdoors to play in the garden
or in a park. Mark out the play area for these games, keeping well
away from any harmful plants or obstacles.*

Follow my
leader

FOLLOW MY LEADER
Age 2 upwards

You will need

*Small obstacles, such as chairs,
buckets, upturned wheelbarrows,
footstools, baskets*

1 Before the game starts, scatter the
obstacles around the play area.
2 The children line up, with an adult
at the front. The adult sets off
around the garden, jumping over or
walking around the obstacles, sitting
down, hopping, skipping, waving
hands in the air, making funny
noises, and so on. All the children
follow and copy the leader.
3 After the first round, the birthday
child can become the leader.

WIBBLY WOBBLY GAME
Age 3 upwards

You will need

*Pieces of chalk or a length
of rope*

1 Divide the children into pairs. If
there is an odd one out, ask a parent
or an adult helper to join in and
partner the child.
2 One partner draws a wavy line on
the ground with a piece of chalk, or
makes a line with a length of rope.
3 The other child tries to walk along
it as if balancing on a tightrope.
4 The partners then swap roles and
repeat the game.

SKITTLES
Age 3 upwards

You will need

Plastic bottles

Piece of string or rope

Foam balls or small potatoes

1 Stand the plastic bottles in a row
and place a piece of string or rope
on the ground a few paces away.
2 Each child stands behind the line
and throws a foam ball or a potato at
the skittles to see how many he can
knock down. The game is over when
everyone has had a turn.

Skittles

MURAL
Age 3 upwards

You will need

...ength of plain paper, or a large white board, and heavy-duty sticky tape

Crayons

Stickers, or pieces of coloured, gummed paper

...Fix the paper or board to a wall ...d put crayons nearby.

...The children can draw around each ...her and colour in the outlines, or ...d gummed paper ...d stickers to make ...tterns on the mural.

ROLL A BALL
Age 3 upwards

You will need

A beach ball

1 The children sit in a circle with legs spread out and feet touching.
2 The birthday child is given the beach ball to start the game. He calls out another child's name and rolls the ball along the floor to her.
3 She then repeats the action. Make sure that every child has a turn.

MAKING BUBBLES
Age 3 upwards

You will need

Bubble mix and a loop for each child

1 Give the children their own bubble mix and loop and show them how to blow bubbles, gently and slowly.
2 See how many bubbles they can make. Can they make giant ones or catch the bubbles they have made? Whose bubble goes the highest?
3 Have spare bubble solution handy.

Mural

OUTDOOR GAMES

These games are more structured and last longer than the games for younger children. Older children may want to play their favourite game several times over, so be prepared!

FREEZE TAG
Age 4 upwards

1 The birthday child is IT first and runs around trying to catch, or to "tag" other players.
2 Anyone who is tagged must "freeze" and stand as still as possible. They cannot move again until another child touches, or "unfreezes", them.
3 Whoever is tagged twice becomes the next IT.
4 When the child playing IT changes, any player who is still frozen can unfreeze. The game starts over again, and each child regains two lives.

DUCK, DUCK, GOOSE
Age 4 upwards

1 The children all sit in a circle. One child is IT and walks around the outside of the circle, gently tapping each child on the head and saying, "duck".
2 Finally, IT taps a player on the head, and says, "goose".
3 The "goose" then has to jump up and chase IT around the circle, trying to catch him before he can reach and sit down in the empty space left by the goose.
4 If IT reaches the space first, the goose becomes the next IT. If the goose catches IT, the same child plays IT again.

PARACHUTE GAME
Age 4 upwards

You will need
An old sheet

1 Gather the children around the edges of the sheet, and ask them to hold on to the edges at intervals.
2 Tell the children to raise the "parachute" up into the air. As it billows up, call out the names of two children.
3 The two children have to run under the sheet and swap places before the parachute comes down.
4 Anyone caught in the parachute can join in again.

DRESSING-UP RACE
Age 4 upwards

You will need

Two piles of clothes (each child will need one item of clothing)

1 Divide the children into two teams. Put the piles of clothes next to each other and a few paces away from the children.
2 Each child has to run to its team's pile of clothes and put on one item of clothing. He or she then runs back to the team.
3 As each child returns to her team, the next one sets off and runs to the pile of clothes. The first team to use up all their clothes wins.

Dressing-up race

ENTERTAINERS

If you are expecting a large number of guests or wish to spend some time talking to other parents, hire an experienced entertainer who can keep the children enthralled.

⚠ CAUTION!
Balloons can be a choking hazard.

Making balloon animals

FINDING AN ENTERTAINER

Some entertainers will run the entire party for you, organizing games and overseeing the meal. Others provide a whole range of separate activities, from puppet shows or face painting to conjuring or balloon modelling.

Entertainers advertise, but it is best to ask around for a personal recommendation. Find someone who is experienced with the age group of the children at your party. Very young children, for instance, may find a heavily disguised clown frightening rather than funny. Bear in mind the following:

◊ Young children have short attention spans. For three-year-olds, make sure that no part of the entertainment lasts for more than

15 minutes. Four- or five-year-olds can concentrate for longer, but they prefer a variety of activities.
◊ If the party has mixed age groups, the entertainer should suit the pace of the youngest children.
◊ Ask what the entertainer does for each age group. Does he or she dress up, organize games, provide balloons or prizes?

Once you have chosen your entertainer, book in advance. Then write to confirm the date, time, and place of the party, your child's age, the number of guests, the party theme if any, your address, and the terms of your agreement. A week beforehand, confirm the booking and ask the entertainer how you should arrange the party area.

HOME ENTERTAINMENT

Why not ask a young friend or relative to put on a magic show by dressing up and performing a few tricks learnt from a book. The birthday child could act as the magician's assistant.

The show could last about 15 minutes

PARTY FOOD

Use a little imagination to tempt small appetites with a feast of savoury and sweet goodies that are tasty, colourful, and fun to eat.

Savoury Treats
An appetising selection of finger foods, dips, open sandwiches, rolls, mini quiches and pizzas, with tips on how to garnish them with pretty patterns or make them look like funny faces, flowers, animals, or toys.

Sweet Treats
A dazzling array of picture biscuits, cakes, and other sweet morsels, fruity desserts and ice-cream sundaes in mouthwatering flavours, as well as home-made summer lollies with real fruit pieces.

Making Cakes
For the crowning glory of the party meal, use these recipes for quick, versatile sponge mixtures and basic icings, then choose from a wealth of original ideas on how to transform plain cakes into magical party cakes.

Drinks
Even children can enjoy their own special cocktails. Here are recipes for exciting fruit-juice punches, creamy milk shakes, and real lemonade.

PARTY FOOD TIPS

◊ To allow time for shopping and preparing the food, plan the party menu a couple of weeks beforehand.

◊ The amount of food depends on the children's age. Small children each need a couple of savoury treats, a pudding, drinks, and cake. For older children, provide each with four savoury treats, two sweet treats, a pudding, drinks, and cake.

◊ Link food into the theme, if you have one. For ideas, see pages 20–27.

◊ Don't forget to cater for parents, if necessary. Provide some savoury nibbles and a fruit punch.

◊ Young children are conservative about food, so keep the basic ingredients simple and concentrate on decoration and presentation.

◊ If you are short of time, buy ready-made food and make it special with garnishes and decoration.

◊ Ask your child if he or she has a preference for a particular type of cake. If not, keep the cake hidden until the party to make it a surprise.

◊ Buy a few favourite small nibbles such as plain crisps and cocktail sausages.

◊ Allow two days for the cake: one day to bake it and the following day to assemble, ice, and decorate it.

◊ Keep portions small. Mini versions of dishes such as pizzas and quiches are fun and easy to eat.

◊ Pour out drinks before the meal and don't leave the jug on the table. Have a cloth handy for spillages. Ask parents of babies and toddlers to bring their own beakers and bottles.

◊ Do not leave matches or knives on the table or within children's reach.

◊ Serve savouries before sweet things and pass around different dishes so that every child has a choice.

◊ Do not worry about how much the children eat. There will always be some who eat nothing but ice cream or crisps at a party.

◊ Add uneaten goodies, such as cupcakes, to going-home party bags.

SAVOURY TREATS

Finger foods are easiest for children to eat at a party. Keep the servings small and be inventive with garnishes - even bread rolls and sandwiches can be made into fun shapes.

OPEN SANDWICHES
Makes 16-24 sandwiches

8 slices BROWN OR WHITE TOAST
4 slices FIRM BREAD, SUCH AS RYE
12 tsp MAYONNAISE OR CREAM CHEESE
About 12 slices each CHEESE AND HAM, OR 24 slices SALAMI

For the garnish

Slices of CUCUMBER, RADISH, OR APPLE; strips of CARROT, PEPPER, OR CHIVES

1 Spread each slice with 1 tsp of mayonnaise or cream cheese.
2 Use pastry cutters to cut out shapes such as stars or animals. Each slice will make 1–2 sandwiches.
3 Cut the slices of cheese, ham, or salami into corresponding shapes. Lay them on top of the bread bases.
4 Make patterns or faces with the garnish ingredients to finish.

SAILBOATS
Makes 12-18 sailboats

1 MEDIUM CUCUMBER
250g (8oz) CREAM CHEESE, OR ANY PICTURE ROLL FILLING (opposite)
3 slices BREAD

1 Cut the cucumber in half lengthways and slice into 4cm (1½in) pieces.
2 Slice off the bottom of each piece. Hollow out the middle and heap in 1 tsp of the chosen filling.
3 Cut each slice of bread into six small triangles to make the "sails".
4 Push a short length of plastic drinking straw through each bread sail, then stick one sail into the filling of each boat.

SAVOURY DIPS
Makes 16-20 servings

500g (1lb) CREAM OR CURD CHEESE
6 tbsp CREAMY YOGURT
SALT AND PEPPER
6 tbsp SMOOTH PEANUT BUTTER

For the finger food

4 CARROTS, ½ CUCUMBER, 1 each RED, YELLOW, AND GREEN PEPPER, 2 CRISP APPLES, 6 BREADSTICKS

1 Mash the cream cheese in a bowl until it is smooth.
2 Mix the yogurt in well. Season to taste.
3 Divide the mixture equally between two bowls. One portion makes a cheese dip.
4 Mix the peanut butter into the other portion to make a peanut butter dip.
5 Cut the vegetables into short strips. Cut the apples into slices and the breadsticks into short lengths to make "fingers".

To serve the dips
1 Divide each dip into two bowls, one for each end of the table.
2 Arrange the vegetable fingers, apple slices, and breadsticks around the bowls. Garnish with a few crisps.

Variations
◊ For tuna dip, replace the peanut butter with 175g (6oz) tinned tuna.
◊ For avocado dip, replace the peanut butter with a mashed avocado.
◊ For tomato dip, replace the peanut butter with 2 tbsp tomato purée or passata.

Open sandwiches

A thick filling like carrot and cheese will support the straw "mast".

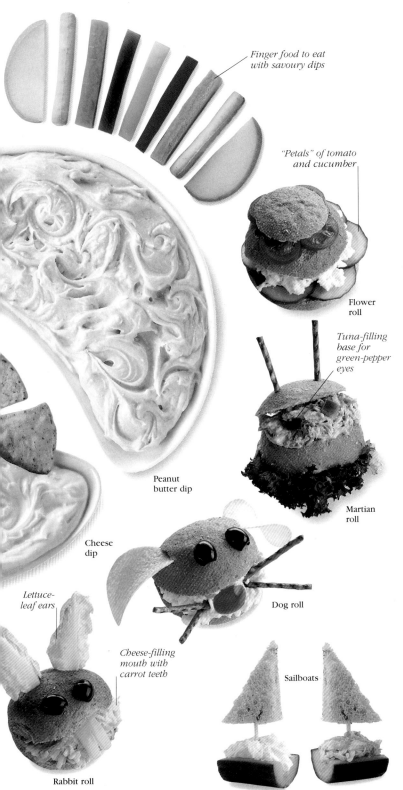

Finger food to eat
with savoury dips

"Petals" of tomato
and cucumber

Flower
roll

Tuna-filling
base for
green-pepper
eyes

Peanut
butter dip

Martian
roll

Cheese
dip

Lettuce-
leaf ears

Dog roll

Cheese-filling
mouth with
carrot teeth

Sailboats

Rabbit roll

PICTURE ROLLS
Makes 18 rolls

18 WHITE OR BROWN BREAD ROLLS

For the fillings

4 EGGS
6 tbsp MAYONNAISE
SALT AND PEPPER
250g (8oz) TIN OF TUNA, DRAINED
175g (6oz) GRATED CHEESE
175g (6oz) GRATED CARROT

For the garnish

CHERRY TOMATOES, CUCUMBER, GREEN
PEPPER, CARROT, SAVOURY STICKS,
STONED OLIVES, LETTUCE, CRISPS

1 For egg mayonnaise filling, boil the eggs for about 10 minutes. Run them under cold water and leave to cool.
2 Remove the shells and mash the eggs in a bowl. Add 2 tbsp of the mayonnaise, season to taste, and stir.
3 For tuna filling, mix the tuna in a bowl with 2 tbsp mayonnaise and add salt and pepper to taste.
4 For carrot and cheese filling, put the grated cheese and carrot and 2 tbsp mayonnaise in a bowl and mix together well. Season to taste.

To assemble the rolls

◊ For a flower, slice into the centre of the roll twice, fill the slices, and garnish with thin slices, or "petals", of cherry tomato and cucumber.
◊ For a Martian, make two cuts into the centre of the roll. Use layers of frilly lettuce to fill the "mouth" at the base of the roll. Fill the top cut and add squares of green pepper for eyes. Put two savoury sticks in the top of the roll to suggest antennae.
◊ For an animal face, cut through the roll almost to the other side. Fill, and decorate with savoury stick whiskers, a halved cherry tomato nose, and carrot teeth. Make four small slits in the top of the roll. Slot in two olive halves for eyes and baby lettuce leaves or large crisps for ears.

SAVOURY TREATS

*Use small pastry cutters and petits fours
cutters to shape these bite-sized savouries
into tempting and amusing nibbles.*

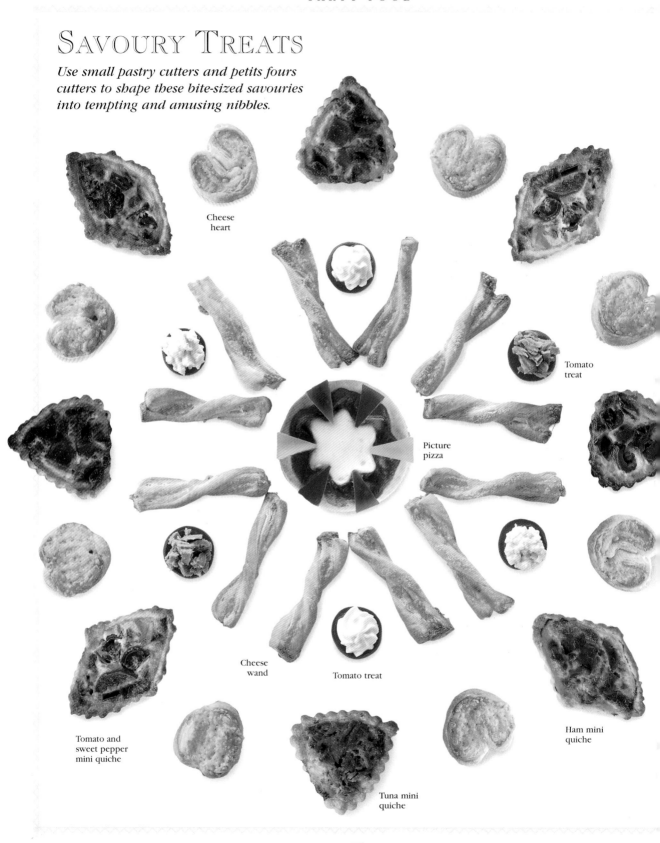

Cheese
heart

Tomato
treat

Picture
pizza

Cheese
wand

Tomato treat

Tomato and
sweet pepper
mini quiche

Tuna mini
quiche

Ham mini
quiche

MINI QUICHES

Makes about 24, using 8cm (3in) tartlet tins

250g (8oz) PLAIN FLOUR
PINCH OF SALT
60g (2oz) BUTTER
60g (2oz) WHITE VEGETABLE FAT
90ml (3fl oz) WATER

For the fillings

GRATED CHEESE, SLICED TOMATOES, CHOPPED SWEET PEPPER OR HAM, TUNA
2 EGGS
300ml (½ pint) SINGLE CREAM
SALT AND PEPPER

Sift the flour and add the salt. Rub in the butter and vegetable fat.
Mix in enough water to make a soft dough. Wrap the dough in kitchen film. Chill in the fridge for 30 minutes.
Roll out the dough on a floured surface. Turn the tartlet tins upside down on the pastry and cut around the shapes, so that the pastry shapes are slightly larger than the tins.
Press the pastry into the greased tins and prick the bases with a fork.
Loosely fill the pastry cases with combinations of your chosen fillings.
Beat the eggs. Whisk in the cream, and add salt and pepper. Pour a little into each pastry case to fill.
Bake for 20 minutes at 200°C/400°F/Gas Mark 6. Leave to cool.

TOMATO TREATS

Makes 20

20 CHERRY TOMATOES
1 quantity EGG MAYONNAISE OR A PICTURE ROLL FILLING (page 55)

Slice a little off the tops and bottoms of the tomatoes, so that they sit flat.
Scoop out some of the seeds and mix with your chosen filling.
Put a teaspoonful of filling into each cherry tomato.

Pizza seal

PICTURE PIZZAS

Makes eight 8cm (3in) pizzas

250g (8oz) SELF-RAISING FLOUR
60g (2oz) BUTTER
½ tsp SALT
125ml (4fl oz) MILK
8 tbsp PASSATA

For the garnish

SLICED MOZZARELLA CHEESE OR GRATED CHEDDAR CHEESE, SLICED HAM, SAUSAGE SLICES, CHOPPED SWEET PEPPERS, HALVED STONED OLIVES

1 Sift the flour and rub it in with the butter and salt in a mixing bowl.
2 Mix in enough milk to make a soft, smooth ball of dough.
3 Roll out the dough in one piece on a floured surface until it is about 6mm (¼in) thick.
4 Cut the dough into 8cm (3in) rounds with a plain pastry cutter. Place the dough bases on a large, greased baking tray.
5 Spread 1 dessertspoon of the passata onto each pizza and cook in the oven at 220°C/425°F/Gas Mark 7 for about 15 minutes.
6 Remove from the oven and make patterns or faces on the tops with the cheese and other garnish ingredients.
7 Grill under a moderate heat until the cheese melts. Leave the pizzas to cool slightly and serve warm.

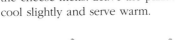

Pastry bites

CHEESY SHAPES

Makes 20 wands and 20-24 hearts

175g (6oz) FROZEN PUFF PASTRY, DEFROSTED
1 BEATEN EGG
175g (6oz) GRATED CHEESE

1 Make the wands: roll out on a floured surface half the pastry into a 13 x 20cm (5 x 8in) rectangle.
2 Brush with beaten egg; sprinkle with 60g (2oz) of the grated cheese.
3 Fold the cheesy pastry in half and roll it into a rectangle again.
4 Cut into strips and twist each strip. Place on a greased baking tray.
5 Make the hearts: roll out the rest of pastry into a 13 x 20cm (5 x 8in) rectangle. Brush with beaten egg.
6 Sprinkle the pastry with 60g (2oz) of grated cheese. Fold over each of the two long edges of the pastry rectangle to meet in the centre.
7 Brush the pastry again with egg. Sprinkle with the remaining cheese.
8 Fold the long outer edges of the pastry into the centre again and press gently together.
9 Cut the roll into 6mm (¼in) slices; lay them on a greased baking tray.
10 Cook all the shapes for 10 minutes at 200°C/400°F/Gas Mark 6 until crisp and golden. Leave to cool.

PASTRY BITES

Makes 30 pastry bites

90g (3oz) FROZEN SHORTCRUST OR PUFF PASTRY, DEFROSTED
1 BEATEN EGG
SESAME SEEDS

1 Roll out the pastry to a 6mm (¼in) thickness and cut into shapes.
2 Brush the pastry shapes with beaten egg and sprinkle half of them with sesame seeds.
3 Put the shapes on a greased baking tray and bake them at 200°C/400°F/Gas Mark 6 for 5–10 minutes until golden brown. Leave to cool.

SWEET TREATS

Combine biscuits and small cakes with fruit dishes and ice cream to create a truly scrumptious spread. Children especially love novelty biscuits and cakes that look like animals and flowers.

Shortbread picture biscuit

PICTURE BISCUITS
Makes 40 biscuits

For plain shortbread mix

| 175g (6oz) PLAIN FLOUR |
| 60g (2oz) CASTER SUGAR |
| 125g (4oz) SOFTENED BUTTER |

For chocolate shortbread mix

| 160g (5½oz) PLAIN FLOUR |
| 15g (½oz) COCOA POWDER |
| 60g (2oz) CASTER SUGAR |
| 125g (4oz) SOFTENED BUTTER |

For the decoration

| ½ QUANTITY OF GLACÉ ICING (right), COLOURED SWEETS |

1 To make each mix, sift the flour and sugar (and cocoa for the chocolate shortbread) into a bowl.
2 Rub in the butter, then knead each mixture gently into a ball of dough.
3 Roll out each dough mixture and press out the biscuit shapes using different-shaped pastry cutters.
4 Bake on greased baking trays at 180°C/350°F/Gas Mark 4 for 15–20 minutes. When the biscuits are cool, decorate with the icing and sweets.

PARTY PRETZELS
Makes 16-20 pretzels

| 125g (4oz) BUTTER |
| 60g (2oz) CASTER SUGAR |
| 1 EGG YOLK, BEATEN |
| 175g (6oz) PLAIN FLOUR |
| PINCH OF SALT |

For the decoration

| 1 EGG WHITE, BEATEN |
| HUNDREDS AND THOUSANDS, CHOCOLATE STRANDS, CHOPPED GLACÉ CHERRIES, PRESERVING SUGAR |

1 Cream together the butter and sugar, beat in the egg yolk, and stir in the flour and salt.
2 Take a heaped teaspoon of the mixture and roll out a sausage shape.
3 Shape the piece of dough into a flower, triangle, or traditional pretzel shape (below).
4 Brush each pretzel with egg white and sprinkle on one of the chosen ingredients for decoration.
5 Place the decorated pretzels on greased baking trays and bake them in the oven at 200°C/400°F/Gas Mark 6 for 10–12 minutes.

Chocolate picture biscuit

Chocolate-sprinkled pretzel

Sugar-coated pretzel

CUPCAKES
Makes 24 cakes or 48 tiny ones

125g (4oz) CASTER SUGAR
125g (4oz) SOFTENED BUTTER
125g (4oz) SELF-RAISING FLOUR
1 tsp BAKING POWDER
2 LARGE EGGS
2–3 drops VANILLA ESSENCE
PINCH OF SALT

For the decoration

GLACÉ ICING (right), COLOURED SWEETS, ANGELICA, CRYSTALLIZED FRUIT

Put all the ingredients in a mixing bowl and beat hard with a wooden spoon until the mixture is smooth. Spoon the mixture into paper cake cases placed in bun tins or, for tiny cupcakes, into paper sweet cases placed on a baking tray.
Bake the cakes in the oven at 190°C/375°F/Gas Mark 5 until they are firm and golden brown. It should take 15–20 minutes for the larger cakes, 10 minutes for the tiny ones. Leave the cakes to cool. Decorate with glacé icing and sweet titbits.

Variations

For chocolate cakes, replace 25g (1oz) flour with the same amount of cocoa powder.
For orange cakes, add grated rind of an orange and 1 tbsp orange juice to the mixture.
For lemon cakes, add grated rind of a lemon and 1 tbsp lemon juice.

CHOCOLATE CRISPIES
Makes 20 cakes or 40 tiny ones

175 g (6oz) PLAIN CHOCOLATE
3 tbsp GOLDEN SYRUP
60g (2oz) SOFTENED BUTTER
175 g (6oz) RICE CRISPIES OR CORN FLAKES
COLOURED SWEETS

1 Break the chocolate into pieces and put in a saucepan. Stir in the syrup and butter over a low heat until all the chocolate has melted.
2 Mix in the breakfast cereal until it is well coated. Spoon the mixture into paper cake cases or sweet cases, press in the sweets and leave to set.

GLACÉ ICING
Makes icing for 20 cupcakes

250g (8oz) ICING SUGAR
About 4 tsp WARM WATER
A few drops FOOD COLOURING

1 Sift the icing sugar into a bowl and mix in water, a little at a time, beating well to make a thick, smooth paste. If the mixture becomes too runny, sift in more icing sugar.
2 To make coloured icing, separate the icing into cups and add a few drops of different-coloured food colouring to each. Remember to leave some of the icing white.
3 Drop a little icing onto a cupcake. Spread it out evenly with the back of a spoon. Pipe different-coloured icing to create faces or patterns.

Chocolate crispie

Iced cupcake

Clown cupcake

Cat cupcake

Butterfly cupcake

Flower cupcake

SWEET TREATS

Brightly coloured fruit treats and ice creams reflect the party mood with a pretty display – and they taste delicious!

SPEEDY FRUIT FOOL
Makes 6

500g (1lb) SOFT FRUIT, e.g., BANANAS, STONED BLACK CHERRIES, KIWI FRUIT, PEACHES, OR STRAWBERRIES

250ml (8fl oz) WHIPPED CREAM

250g (8oz) FROMAGE FRAIS OR CREAMY YOGURT

CASTER SUGAR TO TASTE

For the decoration

SLICED FRUIT

1 Use a fork to mash the fruit in a bowl, then slowly fold in the whipped cream and fromage frais or yogurt.
2 Stir in sugar if needed, and spoon into small bowls or ramekin dishes.
3 To serve, decorate each fool with different slices of fruit.

SUMMER LOLLIES
Makes 6

250ml (8fl oz) FRUIT JUICE, DILUTED BLACKCURRANT SYRUP, OR FRUIT-FLAVOURED YOGURT

280ml (10fl oz) CHOPPED FRESH OR TINNED FRUIT

1 Half-fill plastic lolly moulds with fruit juice, blackcurrant syrup, or yogurt. Freeze for two hours.
2 If using tinned fruit, drain and cut into pieces. Chop up the fresh fruit.
3 Place a little fruit in each lolly mould and use the rest of the juice, syrup, or yogurt to fill the moulds. Put in the sticks and freeze again.
4 Remove the lollies from their moulds by holding them upside-down under warm running water and easing them out.

Arrange fools individually, in a pattern, or as a "foolish bug".

Black cherry fool

Peach fool

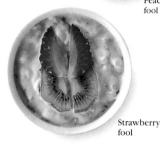
Strawberry fool

Kiwi fruit fool

Banana fool

ICE-CREAM SUNDAES
Makes 8

750ml (24fl oz) ICE CREAM, IN A VARIE OF FLAVOURS AND COLOURS

For the chocolate sauce

125g (4oz) PLAIN CHOCOLATE

150ml (¼ pint) DOUBLE CREAM

2 tsp CASTER SUGAR

150ml (¼ pint) WATER

For the red berry sauce

250g (8oz) FROZEN SUMMER FRUITS

2 tbsp DOUBLE CREAM

4 tbsp ICING SUGAR

1 Scoop tiny balls of ice cream and fill eight small bowls with a selectio
2 Pour chocolate or red berry sauce over each bowl of ice cream.

To make the chocolate sauce
1 Break the chocolate into a bowl over a pan of simmering water. Add the cream, sugar, and water. Stir gently until the chocolate melts.
2 Let the sauce simmer for five minutes, whisking all the time.

To make the red berry sauce
1 Allow the fruits to defrost.
2 Mix all the ingredients together in a blender until you have thick sauce

FRUIT KEBABS
Makes 8

1kg (2lb) COLOURFUL FRUIT SEGMENTS SUCH AS STRAWBERRIES, KIWI FRUIT, PEACHES, TINNED PINEAPPLE, BLACK AND GREEN SEEDLESS GRAPES, STONE CHERRIES, AND MANDARIN ORANGES

1 Halve smaller fruits. Peel and slice larger fruit. Drain tinned fru
2 Thread the pieces of fruit onto short wooden skewers and arrang them on a plate in a fan or circle. Don't use sticks with sharp points.

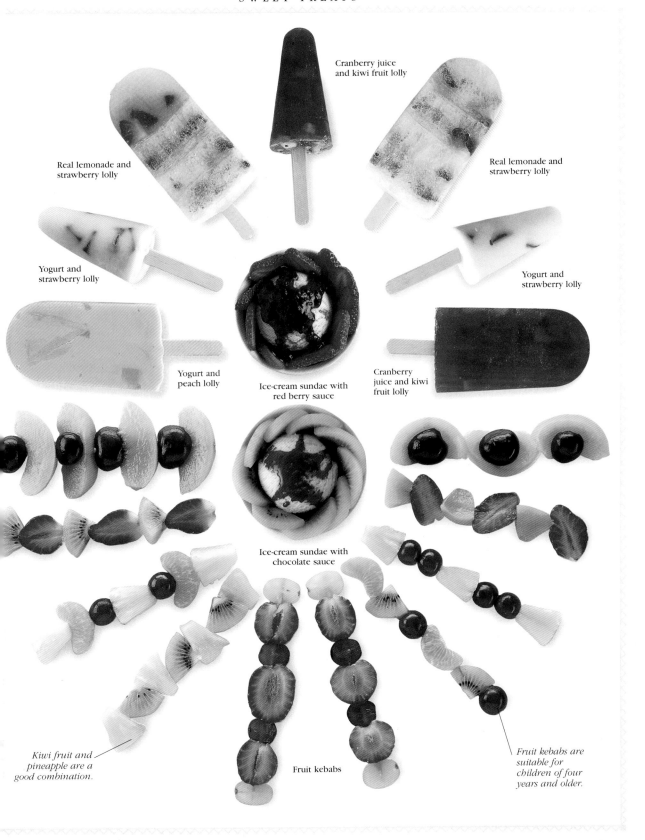

Cranberry juice
and kiwi fruit lolly

Real lemonade and
strawberry lolly

Real lemonade and
strawberry lolly

Yogurt and
strawberry lolly

Yogurt and
strawberry lolly

Yogurt and
peach lolly

Ice-cream sundae with
red berry sauce

Cranberry
juice and kiwi
fruit lolly

Ice-cream sundae with
chocolate sauce

*Kiwi fruit and
pineapple are a
good combination.*

Fruit kebabs

*Fruit kebabs are
suitable for
children of four
years and older.*

MAKING CAKES

*With imaginative shaping and decoration, you can transform
a simple sponge cake like the one shown below into a stunning novelty
centre-piece. Try one of the ideas from the following pages.*

QUICK SPONGE CAKE
Makes 20-24 servings

For a 20cm (8in) round cake

250g (8oz) SOFTENED BUTTER OR MARGARINE
250g (8oz) SELF-RAISING FLOUR, SIFTED
250g (8oz) CASTER SUGAR
4 EGGS
1 tsp BAKING POWDER

For a 20cm (8in) square cake

300g (10oz) SOFTENED BUTTER OR MARGARINE
300g (10oz) SELF-RAISING FLOUR, SIFTED
300g (10oz) CASTER SUGAR
5 EGGS
1½ tsp BAKING POWDER

Quantities

All the recipes given here are for a
sponge mixture to fill a 20cm (8in)
cake tin. As a rule of thumb, if you
want to make a bigger sponge cake,
add one egg and 60g (2oz) each of
flour, butter, and sugar for each
additional 2.5cm (1in) of cake tin.
Increase the quantities of any other
ingredients proportionally.

Variations

◊ For an orange cake, add the juice
and grated zest of one orange (for a
stronger flavour, you can add a little
more zest).
◊ For a lemon cake, add the juice
and grated zest of one lemon (for a
stronger flavour, you can add more
a little more zest).
◊ For a chocolate cake, substitute
30g (1oz) of cocoa powder for the
same amount of flour.

1 Grease the cake tin. Cut some
greaseproof paper to fit the sides,
leaving 2.5cm (1in) extra around the
top. Fringe the edge for a round tin;
cut into the corners for a square tin.

3 Put all the ingredients in a mixing
bowl and beat with a wooden
spoon for about two minutes (or one
minute with an electric mixer) until
the mixture is smooth and creamy.

5 Place the cake on the middle shelf
of the preheated oven. Bake for
1–1¼ hours until the centre of the
cake feels firm and springy.
Let the cake cool for a few
minutes, then turn it over
onto a wire rack. Peel
off the greaseproof
paper. Leave to cool
completely before
decorating.

2 To line the bottom, place the tin
on greaseproof paper and draw
around it. Cut out the circle or square
and press it down into the base of
the tin and smooth it out.

4 Set the oven to 160°C/325°F/Gas
Mark 3. Spoon the mixture into the
cake tin, using a broad-bladed knife
to spread the mixture out to the edge
and to smooth the surface.

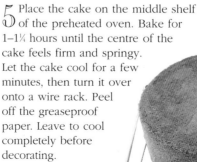

CING THE CAKE

ve different finishes to cakes by using the appropriate
ngs. Choose from fluffy buttercream, glossy glacé
ng, or smooth fondant icing.

BUTTERCREAM ICING

s icing is easy to use and to work
a variety of textures, disguising
face imperfections on the cake. It
he best icing to use on a cake for
y young children.

For a 20cm (8in) cake

125g (4oz) BUTTER OR MARGARINE	
250g (8oz) ICING SUGAR, SIFTED	
2 tsp HOT WATER	

Put the butter or margarine in a
xing bowl and beat with a wooden
oon or electric whisk until soft.
Add the icing sugar and water. Beat
til the icing is pale and creamy.

Variations

For orange or lemon-flavoured
ng, add the finely grated zest of
e orange or lemon.
For chocolate icing, add 15g (½oz)
coa powder and reduce the icing
gar proportionally.
For coloured icing, add food
louring, a few drops at a time.

GLACÉ ICING

is white icing is simple to make,
d spreads evenly.

For a 20cm (8in) cake

125–175g (4–6oz) ICING SUGAR	
1 tbsp WARM WATER	

Sift the icing sugar into a bowl and
x in the water, a little at a time, to
ake a thick, smooth paste. If the
xture becomes too runny, sift in
me more icing sugar.
Spoon the icing onto the cake and
read it out smoothly with the back
a dessertspoon.

FONDANT ICING

Fondant icing is easy to roll out and
gives a smooth, moulded finish to a
cake. You can make your own or
buy ready-made white fondant icing
(also known as sugar paste or ready-
to-roll icing) and add colouring.

For a 20cm (8in) cake

750g (1½lb) ICING SUGAR	
1 LARGE EGG WHITE	
3 tbsp LIQUID GLUCOSE	
A few drops FOOD COLOURING	

1 Sift the icing sugar into a bowl and
make a hollow in the centre.
2 Put the egg white and glucose into
the hollow. Slowly fold the icing
sugar over into the centre until the
mixture is quite stiff.
3 Knead the icing until smooth, and
add the desired amount of food
colouring. Add a little more sugar if
the mixture becomes too soft.
4 Roll out the icing on a surface that
has been lightly dusted with icing
sugar. Lift the icing onto the cake and
mould it around the sides. Trim.

Balls of coloured
fondant icing

Candles

There is a huge range of candles
now available for birthday cakes.
You can choose from classic plain
or spiral shapes and "magic" candles
that you cannot blow out, to single
large candles in the shape of
numerals or cartoon figures. Novelty
candle holders are great fun, too.

DECORATIONS

As well as traditional birthday
candles, you can decorate your
cake with a variety of sweets and
chocolates to create colourful
and realistic pictures.

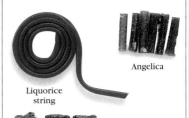

Liquorice
string

Angelica

Chocolate flakes

Milk chocolate
buttons

Hundreds and
thousands

Chocolate
hundreds and
thousands

Candy-covered
chocolate

White chocolate
drops

Chocolate
numbers

Glacé
cherries

Mixed sweets

ROUND CAKES

Adapt round cakes to make any design that includes curves, such as a face, or that forms a geometric shape derived from a circle, like a star.

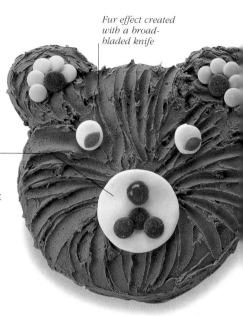

Fur effect created with a broad-bladed knife

Make teddy features from fondant icing, chocolate buttons, and a glacé cherry

TEDDY BEAR CAKE

Makes 20-24 servings

20cm (8in) ROUND CAKE (page 62)
4 CUPCAKES (page 59), UN-ICED
1½ quantities CHOCOLATE BUTTERCREAM ICING (page 63)

For decoration

WHITE AND MILK CHOCOLATE BUTTONS, SMALL AMOUNT OF FONDANT ICING, GLACÉ CHERRY

Use two cupcakes on top of one another for each ear. Cut a small crescent from the side of each so that they sit neatly against the large cake. Paste all the cake sections together with a little icing. Ice and decorate the cake.

DRAGON CAKE

Makes about 20 servings

20cm (8in) ROUND CAKE (page 62)
2 quantities GREEN BUTTERCREAM ICING (page 63)

For decoration

⅓ quantity FONDANT ICING (page 62), ORANGE FOOD COLOURING, 20 WHITE CHOCOLATE DROPS, SMALL BLACK SWEET, COLOURED CARD

KEY

1 Body	3 Tail	5 Jaw
2 Legs	4 Head	6 Spare

1 Cut the sponge cake in half, then cut out the shapes shown above. Discard the spare pieces, or use them to add thickness to the head.

2 Assemble the parts of the dragon as shown above. Using a broad knife, paste the pieces together with icing. Carefully smooth on the rest of the icing, making swirly patterns as you go.

Eye made from fondant icing and a sweet

Flames cut out from coloured card

White chocolate drops for claws and teeth

Orange fondant icing scales

STAR CAKE
Makes about 30 servings

2 x 20cm (8in) ROUND CAKES (page 62)

2 quantities FONDANT ICING (page 63)

A few drops each YELLOW, ORANGE, AND RED FOOD COLOURING

½ quantity BUTTERCREAM ICING (page 63)

This cake is ideal for a big party with parents and relatives, as well as your child's friends. Assemble and ice it on a large cake board or plate. You could make the icing in your child's favourite colours.

CAKE ONE

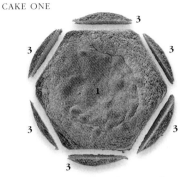

1 Cut off the edges of the circle to make a hexagon. For greater accuracy, draw a template first on baking parchment, then cut around it.

CAKE TWO

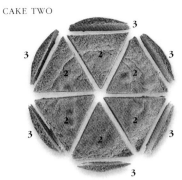

2 Repeat on the second cake. Then make three cuts across the cake, between the six corners. Discard the spare segments from both cakes.

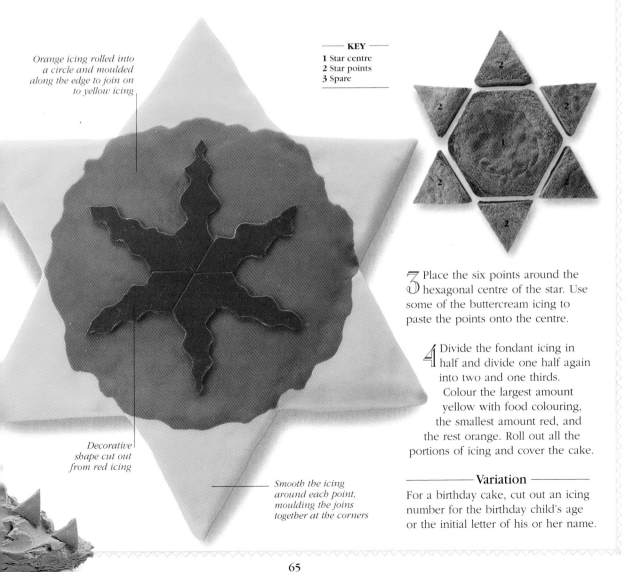

Orange icing rolled into a circle and moulded along the edge to join on to yellow icing

--- **KEY** ---
1 Star centre
2 Star points
3 Spare

Decorative shape cut out from red icing

Smooth the icing around each point, moulding the joins together at the corners

3 Place the six points around the hexagonal centre of the star. Use some of the buttercream icing to paste the points onto the centre.

4 Divide the fondant icing in half and divide one half again into two and one thirds. Colour the largest amount yellow with food colouring, the smallest amount red, and the rest orange. Roll out all the portions of icing and cover the cake.

--- **Variation** ---
For a birthday cake, cut out an icing number for the birthday child's age or the initial letter of his or her name.

SQUARE CAKES

Use basic sponge cakes as building blocks for simple but magical cakes such as the fairy-tale cottage, below, or more elaborate combinations like the train, complete with carriages, on page 69.

FAIRY-TALE COTTAGE

Makes about 36 servings

20cm (8in) SQUARE CHOCOLATE CAKE (page 62)
20cm (8in) SQUARE CAKE (page 62)
1 quantity BUTTERCREAM ICING (page 63)
1½ quantities CHOCOLATE BUTTERCREAM ICING (page 63)

For the decoration

MILK CHOCOLATE DROPS, CHOCOLATE FLAKE, STEM ANGELICA, SUGAR SWEETS, CHOCOLATE MATCHSTICKS, CHOCOLATE NUMBER

1 Cut the square chocolate cake in half, as shown above. These two rectangular pieces will form the base of the cottage.

2 Cut the plain square cake into four triangles, as shown above. These triangular pieces will form the roof of the cottage.

Chimney and tiles suggested by a flake and chocolate drops

Roof ridges made with the flat edge of a broad knife

KEY
1 Cottage base
2 Gable roof

3 Paste the two base sections on top of one another with some chocolate buttercream icing. Paste the roof triangles on their long sides and stand them on top. Trim the edges.

4 Ice the cake with buttercream icing, using the plain icing for the walls and the chocolate icing for the roof. Decorate the cottage.

Windows and door frames of chocolate matchsticks

Cottage garden created from angelica foliage and sugar flowers

NUMBER FOUR CAKE

Makes about 18 servings

20cm (8in) SQUARE CAKE (page 62)

sp APRICOT JAM, MELTED AND SIEVED

quantity YELLOW FONDANT ICING
(page 63)

For the decoration

COLOURED FONDANT ICING SHAPES

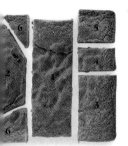

— KEY —
1 Upright
2 Crosspiece
3 Base
4 Upright
   add-on
5 Base add-on
6 Spare

Assemble the pieces, as shown above. Paste the pieces together with the jam as you go. Roll out the fondant icing and mould it around the cake. Decorate with shapes.

Divide the sponge cake into thirds by king two parallel s. Then cut up the rds as shown ove. Discard spare ces.

Shapes cut out from ready-made fondant icing

NUMBER CAKES

A square cake can be cut up in different ways to make a number cake for any age from one to five, as shown below.

— KEY —
1 Upright
2 Base
3 Top
4 Corner

— KEY —
1 Base
2 Middle
3 Top
White areas
are spare

— KEY —
1 Base
2 Middle
3 Top
White areas
are spare

— KEY —
1 Top
2 Middle
3 Base
White areas
are spare

SQUARE CAKES

WIZARD'S HAT CAKE
Makes about 20 servings

20cm (8in) SQUARE CAKE (page 62)
4 tbsp APRICOT JAM, MELTED AND SIEVED
1 quantity FONDANT ICING (page 63)
A few drops PURPLE FOOD COLOURING

Moon and star pastry cutters

1 Cut the cake into three triangular shapes, as above. Use jam to paste the two smaller pieces on top of the large triangle. Round off the edges and top with a knife.

2 Keep a small portion of the icing for decoration. Colour the rest purple, roll out, and cover the cake with it. Roll out the white icing and cut out star and moon shapes with pastry cutters.

Cargoes of sweets fill the carriages

Lay down liquorice strings for the rail tracks

Mini biscuits make good carriage wheels

Train on a track
If you want to make an even longer train, use the spare pieces of cake to make another carriage. You could also add gingerbread passengers and crew.

TRAIN CAKE

2 x 20cm (8in) SQUARE CHOCOLATE
CAKES (page 62)

¼ quantity BUTTERCREAM ICING
(page 63)

[t]sp APRICOT JAM, MELTED AND SIEVED

450g (1lb) RED FONDANT ICING
(page 63)

[3]00g (10oz) BROWN FONDANT ICING

For the decoration

¼ quantity PLAIN SHORTBREAD
MIXTURE (page 58)

[¼] quantity CHOCOLATE SHORTBREAD
MIXTURE (page 58)

2 CHOCOLATE FINGERS,
[C]HOCOLATE BISCUIT, 8 MINI BISCUITS,
2 RED LIQUORICE STRINGS,
2 GLACÉ CHERRIES, SWEETS

KEY	
1 Carriages	**4** Engine front
2 Engine base	**5** Spare
3 Engine cab	

CAKE ONE

1 Cut the first cake in half, then cut
out the smaller pieces, as shown
above. These pieces make the train
carriages and part of the engine cab.

3 Cut the two squares (1) for the
carriages in half horizontally. Cut
a rectangle out of the centre of each
top half. Paste the top and bottom
layers of each carriage together
with a layer of buttercream icing.

CAKE TWO

2 Cut the second cake in half, then
cut up one half again, as shown
above. These pieces will form most
of the engine cab.

4 Trim the other pieces so that they
are level on top. Paste the layers
together, as shown above, with jam.
Roll out the icing; cover the carriages
and engine front with red icing and
the rest with brown icing. Decorate.

Spiral Biscuits

To make four spiral biscuits for the
wheels, roll each shortbread dough
mix into an 8 x 10cm (3 x 4in)
rectangle. Lay the chocolate
dough on top of the plain.
Press to firm and roll up into
a sausage. Cut into 1cm
(½in) slices. Bake as for
picture biscuits (page 58).

[Fo]ndant
icing
[w]indow

*Brown
fondant icing
chimneys*

*Glacé cherries for
headlights*

*Chocolate
biscuit
buffer*

*Spiral
biscuit
wheel*

*Chocolate
matchstick axle*

DRINKS

You can make wonderful drinks just by mixing different fruit juices. Experiment with combinations of flavours, remembering that fruit drinks for very young children should be diluted.

RUBY FRUIT PUNCH
Makes 1.8 litres (3 pints)

1.2 litres (2 pints) FIZZY LEMONADE

0.6 litre (1 pint) RED GRAPE JUICE

For decoration
PURPLE SEEDLESS GRAPES

1 Mix the fizzy lemonade and red grape juice together.
2 Serve chilled, with grapes.

CHOCO-MILK
Makes 1.8 litres (3 pints)

3 tbsp CHOCOLATE DRINKING POWDER

1.8 litres (3 pints) MILK

For decoration
GRATED CHOCOLATE

1 Mix the chocolate powder into a smooth paste in a little milk. Mix in a blender with the rest of the milk.
2 Sprinkle with grated chocolate.

RED POTION
Makes 3.75 litres (6 pints)

1.2 litres (2 pints) each APPLE JUICE, CRANBERRY JUICE, AND SPARKLING MINERAL WATER OR FIZZY LEMONAD

For decoration
APPLE OR CRANBERRY CRUSHED ICE

1 Mix all the juices together.
2 Serve with flavoured crushed ice.

Add a decorated straw to make a fun drink

Ruby fruit punch

Choco-milk

Red potion

SUNSET PUNCH
Makes 3.75 litres (6 pints)

.2 litres (2 pints) each ORANGE JUICE, PINEAPPLE JUICE, AND PEACH JUICE

For decoration

PINEAPPLE JUICE CRUSHED ICE, PEACH SLICES

Mix all the juices together. Serve with crushed ice and a peach ce on the edge of the glass.

--------- **Variation** ---------

For a sunrise punch, use 1.8 litres (3 pints) each of orange juice and fizzy lemonade.

Sunset punch

STRAWBERRY SHAKE
Makes about 1.8 litres (3 pints)

1.2 litres (2 pints) MILK
375g (12oz) STRAWBERRIES
4 tbsp SOFT BROWN SUGAR
4 scoops VANILLA ICE CREAM
250g (8oz) NATURAL YOGURT

For decoration

WHOLE STRAWBERRIES

1 Put half the amount of each ingredient in a blender and mix for 40 seconds, until thick and frothy.
2 Repeat with the rest of the ingredients.
3 Decorate.

Strawberry shake

REAL LEMONADE
Makes 1.8 litres (3 pints)

6 LARGE LEMONS
150g (5oz) SUGAR
1.5 litres (2½ pints) WATER

1 Wash the lemons and finely peel the zest from three of them. Put the zest in a large bowl.
2 Add the juice of all six lemons and the sugar. Boil the water and stir into the lemon mixture.
3 Leave overnight in a cool place, so that the flavour is fully infused.
4 Check that the lemonade is sweet enough and add more sugar if necessary. Strain through a sieve to remove the zest before serving.

⚠ CAUTION!
Use plastic glasses for young children.

Real lemonade

FIRST AID

This section covers the basic first aid needed to deal with the minor mishaps, and occasional crises, that may occur when a number of children play together.

Cuts and Grazes	Foreign Body in the Eye
Nosebleed	Vomiting
Severe Bleeding	Poisoning
Splinter	Asthma
Stings	Choking

FIRST-AID TIPS

It is unlikely that you will have to deal with a serious accident while supervising a children's party, but the antics of a group of exuberant children may result in a child suffering a nosebleed or a grazed knee. If a child who has a condition such as asthma becomes over-excited, he might suffer an attack. An injured child may over-react because of the unfamiliar people and environment, so reassure him while you assess the injury. Leave an adult in charge of the group while you tend to the child.

If the child has suffered a very minor injury, such as a graze, let him rejoin the party when he likes, and tell the parents what happened when they collect him. If the condition is more serious, or the child is very upset, call the parents, and if necessary an ambulance, straightaway.

First-Aid Kit

It is advisable to keep a first-aid box accessible at home. Buy a standard family kit or put together your own. You could also buy a standard kit and add a few extra articles of your own. Always keep any medicines locked away. A well-stocked first-aid kit could include the following.

◊ 1 small roller bandage
◊ 1 large roller bandage
◊ 1 small conforming bandage
◊ 1 large conforming bandage
(conforming bandages mould themselves
to the shape of the body)
◊ 2 eye pads with bandages
◊ scissors
◊ calamine cream or lotion
◊ pack of gauze swabs
◊ 2 triangular bandages
(good for slings)
◊ hypoallergenic tape
◊ 2 sterile pads
◊ waterproof plasters
◊ 1 finger bandage and applicator
◊ tweezers
◊ 1 sterile dressing with bandage

If you don't have the right equipment, adapt a few household items for first-aid situations. For instance, use a bag of ice or frozen peas wrapped in a cloth as a cold compress to reduce swelling. If you need to make a sling or cover a burn, a clean pillowcase will serve the purpose. Some children are allergic to plasters, so check with the parents before the party. If a child has an allergy, use a non-adhesive dressing with a pad. Always keep a variety of plasters and dressings. Plasters with cartoon designs are good because they distract the child.

CUTS AND GRAZES

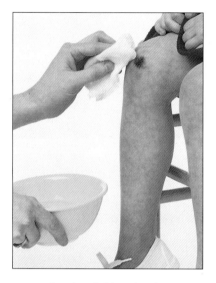

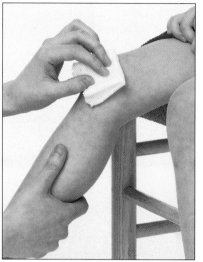

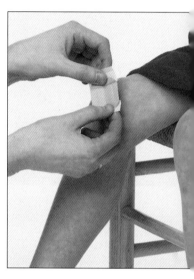

1 Comfort the child and sit her down. Use a gauze pad soaked in warm water or a very soft brush to wash the wound gently. Use a fresh pad for each wipe. Try to remove any loose particles of gravel or dirt. This may cause a little new bleeding.

2 Pat the area dry with clean gauze or a lint-free cloth. Don't use cotton wool or anything else that might stick to the wound and delay healing. Press firmly with a clean pad to stop the bleeding. If the wound bleeds excessively, see box, below.

3 Dress the cut or graze with a plaster that has a pad large enough to cover the wound and the area around it, or use a non-adhesive bandage with a sterile pad. Tell the child's parents about the mishap when they collect the child.

NOSEBLEED

Breathing through his mouth will calm him down

1 Sit the child down and help him to lean over a bowl with his head tilted forward. Tell him to breathe through his mouth. Gently pinch his nostrils together, just below the bridge of his nose, for ten minutes.

2 Ask the child to spit out any excess fluid in his mouth. If the bleeding goes on after ten minutes, pinch his nose for another ten minutes. Release the pressure. If his nose is still bleeding, repeat the procedure.

IF the nosebleed lasts thirty minutes or more, or the discharge is thin and watery, take the child to hospital and notify his parents.

3 Once the bleeding stops, clean around the child's mouth and nose with cotton wool dipped in warm water. Don't let him pick at, or blow, his nose, or it may bleed again.

4 Keep the child quiet for half an hour before he rejoins the party, and tell his parents about the nosebleed when they collect him.

SEVERE BLEEDING

Press firmly on the wound with a clean pad. Lay the child down; keep the wound raised above her heart for ten minutes. Bandage the pad in place firmly, but not tightly. If blood seeps through, put another pad on top. Call the parents; take the child to hospital.

PLINTER

Clean the area around the splinter with soap and warm water.

Do not try to remove the splinter with a needle. Sterilize a pair of weezers by passing them through a me. Let the tweezers cool. Don't uch the ends or wipe off the soot.

Support the child's hand. With the tweezers, grasp the splinter as ose to the skin as possible. Draw it the splinter at the angle it went in.

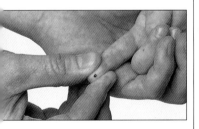

Squeeze the wound so it bleeds a little, to flush out any dirt. Wash e area again and pat it dry. Cover e wound with a plaster or a non-lhesive bandage. Let the parents now when they collect the child.

the splinter breaks or will not ome out easily, call a doctor and the arents. A doctor will advise whether e child needs a tetanus inoculation.

STING

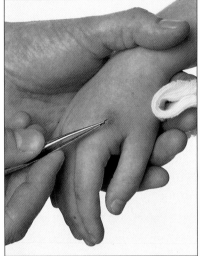

1 If the child is stung by a bee or wasp and the sting is in the skin, grasp it with tweezers as close to the skin as possible and pull it out. Don't squeeze the top of the sting – you may force poison into the wound.

2 Cool the area with a cloth wrung out in cold water. Leave the compress in place until the swelling subsides and the pain is relieved. Rest the injured part. Tell the parents when they collect the child.

IF the child develops breathing difficulties, or collapses, following a sting, she may be having an allergic reaction. Call an ambulance immediately. Then call her parents.

STING IN THE MOUTH

If a child is stung in the mouth, call her parents and a doctor. Give her cold water to drink or an ice cube to suck. This will keep down any swelling in the mouth that could lead to breathing difficulties. If she does find breathing difficult, call an ambulance at once.

Watch the child until the doctor arrives.

FOREIGN BODY IN THE EYE

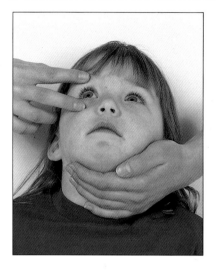
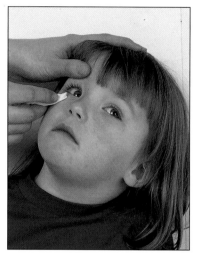
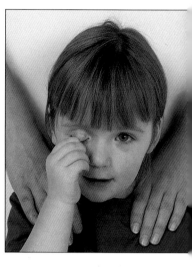

1 Stop the child rubbing her eye. Sit her down so that she is facing the light and tilt her head back. Carefully separate the eyelids. Ask her to look right, left, and up and down so that you can examine all the eye surface.

2 If you can see the foreign body, use a damp swab or handkerchief to lift it out. Alternatively, tilt her head and pour clean water towards the inner corner of the eye so that the water washes over the eye.

3 If an object is under the eyelid, ask an older child to clear it by lifting her upper eyelid over the lower one. If the child is too young, do it for her, but wrap her in a towel to stop her pulling at your arms.

VOMITING

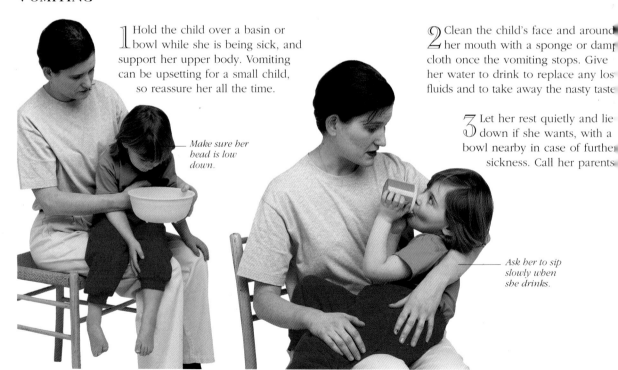

1 Hold the child over a basin or bowl while she is being sick, and support her upper body. Vomiting can be upsetting for a small child, so reassure her all the time.

Make sure her head is low down.

2 Clean the child's face and around her mouth with a sponge or damp cloth once the vomiting stops. Give her water to drink to replace any lost fluids and to take away the nasty taste.

3 Let her rest quietly and lie down if she wants, with a bowl nearby in case of further sickness. Call her parents.

Ask her to sip slowly when she drinks.

POISONING

3 If he has swallowed chemicals, wipe away any residue from his face and give him sips of cold water or milk to drink. Keep the containers to show to the doctor.

4 Never try to make the child sick, as this can cause him further harm. If he is sick anyway, keep a sample to show to the doctor.

5 Call the doctor or an ambulance immediately and tell them which poison is involved, if you know. Lay the child down to rest. Call the parents and keep an eye on the child until the ambulance arrives.

1 If you think a child has swallowed anything poisonous, such as drugs, household chemicals, alcohol, or part of a plant, keep calm and try to find out from the child what he has taken, when he took it, and how much.

2 If the child has eaten something, look inside his mouth. With a finger, hook out any plant pieces, berries, or pills you can see. Keep samples for the doctor. If the child has taken drugs, keep the container.

ASTHMA

Symptoms:
- Difficulty in breathing
- Blue tinge to face and lips
- Anxiety and distress
- Coughing
- Wheezing when breathing out

If a child has an inhaler, he will probably know how to use it.

Sit her forwards with her arms resting on a table.

1 Take the child to a well-ventilated and smoke-free room and encourage her to relax. Sit her down at a table or on your lap. Ask the child to lean forward in order to ease her breathing. Reassure the child.

2 If the child has special medication or an inhaler, make sure that he uses it straightaway. Let the child rest until the attack has eased and tell the parents when they collect him.

IF you suspect this is the child's first attack, call the parents and a doctor. If the attack is severe, call an ambulance.

CHOKING

⚠ CAUTION!
*See notes in
italics for first aid
for babies.*

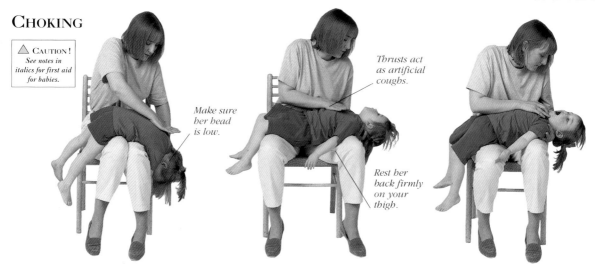

*Make sure
her head
is low.*

*Thrusts act
as artificial
coughs.*

*Rest her
back firmly
on your
thigh.*

1 If a child is choking, ask her to cough. If she cannot cough up the obstruction, quickly bend her over your knees (*lay a baby along your forearm*). Give five sharp slaps between the shoulder-blades.

2 If back slaps fail, turn her over on your knees (*turn a baby face up on your arm*). Put the heel of one hand (*for a baby, use two fingers*) on her lower breastbone. Give five sharp downward thrusts.

4 If she is still choking, put the heel of one hand just below the ribs in the middle of the upper abdomen and give five firm, upward thrusts (*NEVER do this on a baby*).

3 Check the child's mouth to see if the blockage has cleared. Press her tongue down with a finger for a clear view. If you see an object, hook it out with a finger, but don't put a finger blindly down her throat.

5 Check her mouth (step 3). If the blockage has not cleared, call an ambulance. Repeat steps 1–4 (*1–3 for a baby*) until help arrives or the blockage clears. Call the parents.

IF the child falls unconscious, her throat may relax and she may start to breathe. If not, give artificial ventilation (call the ambulance service for instructions).

FOR A LARGER CHILD

If the choking child is a tall four- or five-year-old and too big to lay on your lap, make her stand up and bend forward while you give her five back slaps. Lay her on the floor if you give chest and abdominal thrusts (right).

If you need to give back slaps again once the child is lying on the floor, gently roll her over onto her side so that she is facing towards you.

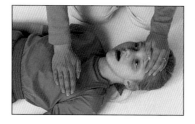

1 After giving the first five back slaps, lay the child on her back, and give five downward chest thrusts. Check her mouth for any obstruction.

2 If the blockage hasn't cleared, give five abdominal thrusts. Check the child's mouth again. If this fails, call an ambulance, and repeat the steps until help arrives.

PLANNING CHECKLIST

Use this checklist to help you prepare for your child's party well in advance. Tackle the tasks in stages over the preceding weeks to avoid a last-minute rush and unnecessary confusion.

Two months or more before

◊ Visit and choose a party venue, if required. Book the venue and confirm the booking in writing.
◊ Book an entertainer, if required, and confirm in writing.

Three to four weeks before

◊ Draw up a guest list.
◊ Decide on a party theme, if any.
◊ Buy or make invitations and buy suitably sized envelopes.
◊ Send out invitations.
◊ Arrange for a friend (or friends) to help you with the party
◊ Ask a friend to prepare a magic show, if required.

Two weeks before

◊ Write out a party plan.
◊ Plan the decorations, menu, games or activities, treats or prizes.
◊ Draw up lists of all the items you need to buy or make.
◊ Shop for the decorations or any materials needed to make them, paper table decorations, props for activities or games, toys and novelties for prizes and treats, camera or video film.

One week before

◊ Ring to confirm bookings of party venue and entertainer, if needed.
◊ Ring parents of any guests who have not replied to the invitations.
◊ Make decorations, masks, hats, party bags, prize chest, or medals.
◊ Buy basic ingredients for any food to be prepared in advance.

Two days before

◊ Check your lists to see that you have everything you need.
◊ Do final food shopping.
◊ Make the birthday cake.
◊ For an outdoor party, clear any hazards from the garden.
◊ Put activities' materials and games' props in boxes in order of play.
◊ Fill party bags, wrap treats, or fill a prize chest; put in a safe place.

One day before

◊ Make any savoury or sweet treats. Let them cool, then decorate them if needed. Store pastries in airtight containers. Ice the cake.
◊ Prepare and refrigerate sandwich fillings, dips, and lollies.
◊ Prepare food for adult guests.

Party day

◊ Pin up the party plan in an obvious place.
◊ Clear and decorate the rooms where the party is to be held, or decorate the party venue.
◊ Blow up balloons. Decorate them if required, and hang them up out of reach of the children.
◊ Put out the props for the games and activities, and set out toys and books or outdoor play equipment.
◊ Put the party bags, treats, or going-home presents in a handy place.
◊ Assemble the sandwiches, rolls, or sailboats. Grill sausages, make pizzas or tomato treats, and prepare any fruit desserts or sundaes. Arrange all the food on serving dishes and plates and refrigerate.
◊ Prepare the drinks and refrigerate.
◊ Decorate and lay the table.
◊ Lock stair or garden gates and block off out-of-bounds areas.
◊ Put tape or film in the camcorder or camera and put somewhere safe.
◊ Dress the family in their party clothes, take a deep breath, and prepare to greet the guests!

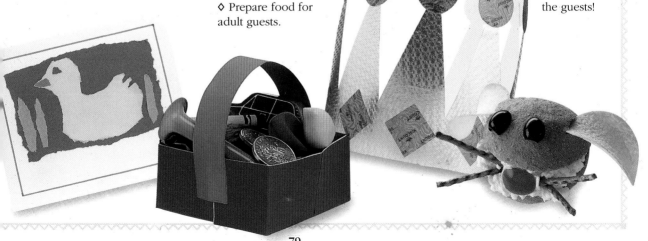

INDEX

ACKNOWLEDGMENTS

The author would like to thank
Beata Nagel-Petry for the loan of her books; Carol Watson for her
help with research on party games.

Dorling Kindersley would like to thank
Jane Bull for designing and assembling party decorations,
invitations and props; Nick Goodall for photographic assistance;
Nicola Hill and Lisa Minsky for editorial assistance; Barbara Owen
for supplying costumes, Jessica Bennett and Annette Sullivan for
design assistance; and the following for modelling:
CHILDREN: Roshi Bell, Billy and Charlotte Bull, Michael Campbell,

James Courtenay Clack, Ashan Craig, Kelia and Keris Cuyun
Evans, Austin Enil, Amy Fuller, Anna and Thomas Greene, Lauren
Greene, Pippa Hill, James Lynch, Alex and Gina McHarg, Maija
Marsh, Hayley Miles, Chlöe and Freddie Mitchell, Rowan Page,
Finn Shannon, Tarahumara Diaz Silva, Natalie Thomas, Ryan
Thomas, Amy Beth Walton, and Sam Whiteley;
ADULTS: Stephen Bull and Caroline Greene.

Home economists: Kathy Mann and Jenny Shapter.

Index: Hilary Bird.